MATER SPIRITUALIS

THE LIFE OF ADELHEID OF VILICH

by Madelyn Bergen Dick

Illustrations by Alison Brown

PEREGRINA PUBLISHING CO.

Toronto, Ontario

Peregrina Translations Series no. 19
ISSN 0832-7092

ISBN 0-920669-48-4

Peregrina Publishing Co.
49 Front Street East, Second Floor
Toronto, Ontario M5E 1B3

Printed and bound in Canada
by Hignell Printing Co.
Winnipeg, Manitoba

IN MEMORIAM

Paul Werner Bergen, *pater*

Hans Knorr, *magister*

Adelheid of Vilich
British Library, Harl. 2800, fol. 207ᵛ (sæc. XIII)
Reproduced by permission of the British Library

Contents

Vilich Abbey Church
1990

Introduction

I N THE FALL OF 1987 I WENT ON A PILGRIMAGE—NOT THE SORT that seeks out shrines and relics, but rather a pilgrimage to an historic time and place. With the aid of a detailed map and a rented Opel Kadett, I met the challenge of a horrendous network of modern highways and ancient roads. Thus I travelled through the Rhineland, particularly the area between Cologne and Koblenz. I set out to find not the modern landscape but the mediæval one, to locate the places that existed in this land more than nine hundred years ago.

Historians usually search for people's lives and the impact of these lives in the surviving written records of the past. In these pages of vellum we find the recorded incidents that bring long forgotten men and women alive: their quests, their worries, their loves and their hates are there for us to study and to ponder. But these stories become meaningless if we do not understand their context. We must see them against the background of their times; we must most assuredly see them in the context of their places.

That autumn, I was searching for the context of time and place in the lives of Count Otto of Hammerstein and his wife Irmingard. It had been easy to find their times. For the last hundred years, historians have studied the turbulent story of their divorce, desired by emperor and clergy, and their love, passionately asserted by themselves. Even their contemporaries were well aware of their story: Thietmar of Merseburg in his *Chronicon* devoted several paragraphs to the passions of his distant kinsman.

It was not so easy to find their place. The Rhineland area between Cologne and Koblenz has seen much history: the incredible growth in population as well as numerous wars with their armies of destruction had altered the landscape beyond recognition. But I was on a pilgrimage and as every good and faithful pilgrim knows, the holy places are not easily reached. I looked at maps. I asked long-time residents for clues and I imagined myself back into the Hammersteiner time. And I found their "place."

The rock upon which their fortress had stood still rises steeply and broodingly on the eastern bank of the Rhine and the river, broad and prone to flooding, runs just as swiftly at its base as it did in the fall of 1020. A hundred years later a new Hammerstein family would take possession of the site and expand the existing royal keep. In the seventeenth century that castle was destroyed by Flemish mercenaries but the site is still owned by the descendants of the late mediæval family. Along the steep slopes of the Hammerstein where it faces the river are vineyards, and at the northward base are the villages of Niederhammerstein and Oberhammerstein, tiny communities squeezed between the river and the mountain, which owe their existence to the green grapes in the vineyards and the crisp white wine that is made from them.

I ascended that steep slope on a cold and partly cloudy October day and walked through the vineyards, then through a meadow and finally up a slippery-wet narrow path which led to the top and the castle ruins. On my way up I could see the broad slopes going down the east side of the Hammerstein, now overgrown with trees and underbrush, which the army of Henry II must have scaled. Through four long months the count and his lady defied the emperor and when it was all over—on December 26, 1020, the day of St. Stephen the first Christian martyr—the loving couple, beaten by hunger, were outlaws on their own lands, their home a smoking ruin. The Emperor who had spent much time and energy on their defeat, quickly came to realise that he had gained little by it. To the end of his reign in 1024, they would defy his might and that of the Archbishop of Mainz; their loyalty and their love would conquer all obstacles in the end.

Standing on the river side of their high place, as they must have stood, I found myself breathless before the view that unfolded below me. The road, a narrow, winding ribbon, looked insignificant from above; the river Rhine dominated the landscape. When the sun made a brief appearance through clouds and mist, time past and time present coalesced and one part of my pilgrimage was complete.

The Hammerstein was the end of my initial journey; it was not, however, its beginning. Through my research of the written records of the lives of Otto and Irmingard, I had come across a *vita*, written the middle of the eleventh century by a nun called Bertha about the first abbess of her convent. In the description of the abbess' family are located the origins of my loving couple and some of the reasons why the legality of their marriage was challenged. In the tangled web of a family history I read about the grandparents, mother, aunts, and cousins of Count Otto and by inference the family connection to his wife which had exercised and antagonised the archbishops Erkenbald and Aribo of Mainz as well as the Emperor Henry II.

The *vita*, describing events several decades earlier than the siege of the Hammerstein, also had a place. It proved far easier to find than the bleak Hammerstein, for the church of the convent, where that abbess had lived, still dominated the smooth flood plains of the eastern banks of the Rhine, as it must have done throughout the Middle Ages.

So I drove on the narrow road away from the Hammerstein through small towns; I ignored the mighty bridges going west over the Rhine to Bonn, and briefly joined the *Autobahn* that runs from Frankfurt to Cologne and Düsseldorf. In no time at all I found myself in Beuel, a large trans-river suburb of Bonn. Hidden in this conglomerate of small towns is the *Ortsteil* Vilich: Vilich was also the name of the convent I had come to see.

The abbey of Vilich was founded in c. 980 A.D. by Megengoz and his wife Gerberga and their youngest daughter, Adelheid, became its first abbess. The founders built the original abbey church and the convent. They also procured a charter of immunities modeled on those of the great imperial abbeys from the seven-year old Emperor Otto III and his mother, the Dowager-Empress Theophanu, though their convent was neither important nor large. The *vita* does not give the reasons why so small a foundation should have such high imperial approval but it did give details of the five children of Megengoz and Gerberga. A son called Godfrey died on the Slavic frontier in 977; two daughters were nuns, and two daughters were married and had children. One of the married daughters, Irmintrud/ Imiza, was a close friend of the Dowager-Empress. It was thus entirely possible that a royal patron rewarded a loyal friend as well as honouring a warrior fallen in battle, thereby helping a grieving family to built a monument to a lost son.

The little abbey survived until its secularisation in the first decade of the nineteenth century. The church was rebuilt at least three times in the Middle Ages and twice in the seventeenth century. After extensive war-damage in this century, a team of historians and archeologists carefully examined the structures and its secrets in the late 1950's and restored the building to its thirteenth-century interior. Today the Church, dedicated to St. Peter, stands as a beacon on the flat land; its pale pink stucco walls can glow like lustre in the late autumn sunlight.

After I had visited Vilich, the second part of my pilgrimage was completed. I had gone in search of a war-like count and his beloved wife; I had also found a saintly abbess and her church. And yes, the two halves of my journey are connected: Count Otto of Hammerstein was the nephew of the Abbess Adelheid, and the son of the Lady Imiza whose friendship with an empress had set a community of pious nuns on a path that was to last for more than eight hundred years.

There is a footnote to my pilgrimage, another place which I visited that fall of 1987, this time accompanied by my cousin. This place was the *Staatsarchiv* of the Province of Nordrhein-Westfalen in Düsseldorf. Many of the charters and other papers of the Abbey of Vilich, which once must have been amongst its most treasured possessions, are housed in these provincial archives. After a long wait caused by a problem with a light-bulb and the absence of a flashlight, the documents were brought from the cellar by a member of the staff. My cousin, a medical doctor, and I, a mediæval historian, called upon our knowledge of Latin and mediæval paleography and read ancient parchments that told the story of the foundation of Vilich: the Charter of 944 by Otto I pardoning Adelheid's father Megengoz for his rebellion and returning his lands; the Otto III foundation charter of 987; the eleventh-century copy of the 996 charter of Pope Gregory V, the thirteenth-century copy of Henry II's 1003 reaffirmation of Vilich's immunities, which named Adelheid as the Abbess. We whispered softly in the reading room and felt that the centuries, indeed a millennium, could truly be forgotten. The words and the physical presence of those parchments brought us very close to those people whose deeds were recorded there.

The translation of the *Vita Adelheidis* (Chapter 1 of this book) and the four chapters discussing issues arising from this source are the results of my research and my pilgrimage. The translation is not a word-for-word rendition of the Latin nor an attempt to reproduce the rhymed prose which Bertha used for her work. Rather, without sacrificing accuracy of vocabulary, syntax, and rhetorical convention, I have retold Bertha's *vita* in the most accessible English to which the text lends itself. If I have erred on the side of English style and modern usage rather than produce a literal translation, I have done so with clear intent. For those reading my efforts, I hope that I have conveyed a true sense of the late tenth and early eleventh century, both in the English version of the text and in my discussions; for those who wish to read the words as Bertha wrote them in 1057, they can be found in the *Monumenta Germaniae historica Scriptores,* XV or in Achter's *Die Stiftskirche St. Peter in Vilich.* The two surviving mediæval manuscripts are located in the Royal Library in Brussels and in the British Museum in London.

I would like to take this opportunity to thank all the people who have helped me in the research and writing of this book: to my uncle and cousin in Germany for assistance in finding my way around an unfamiliar landscape, to colleagues at the University of the Ruhr for the use of their library; to the librarians in the Interlibrary-Loan Department at York University who worked tirelessly to obtain obscure volumes for me from

Germany. Special thanks goes to my son, Alexander, who read and corrected the translation and spent hours listening to me discuss mediæval Latin literature and to Alison Brown who made these sketches of the Vilich abbey church. Finally, a word of thanks to my students who studied the *vita* with me, to my friends who never tired of listening to me spout off on eleventh-century nunneries, and to my husband who climbed the Hammerstein ruins with me and drove through the French and Belgian country-sides to find out more about the wide-flung connections of the Vilich family.

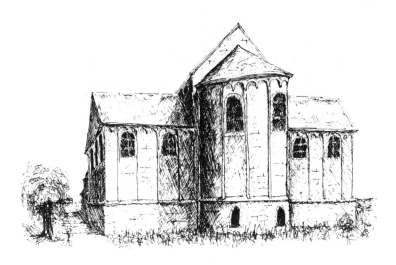

Vilich Abbey Church
c. 1000
[Artist's rendition]

Vita Adelheidis
British Library, Harl. 2800, fol. 207ᵛ (sæc. XIII)
Reproduced by permission of the British Library

1 The Source: The Life of Adelheid, Abbess of Vilich, by Bertha

Prologue

T O THE LORD ARCHBISHOP ANNO, VENERATED, BELOVED OF ALL Christians, a poor and miserable sinner, not worthy to be called his servant, wishes blessings of eternal joy upon the end of this tedious life. Encouraged by the example of the Patriarch Abraham who several times dared to approach God as a friend,[1] so will I turn to address you, my Lord, the faithful imitator of that powerful God. In humility I implore your grace, so that in the name of him who preferred the mite of the widow to the uncountable gifts of the wealthy, this plain work may be a pleasing gift to your Highness. May it remind you not to forget the requests of your poor servant, so that through the intercession of that holy Virgin, whose merits are herein described, all those things, which have failed through your human weaknesses, might be effaced.

HERE BEGINS THE LIFE

CHAPTER ONE

We call you, Father and Lord, most revered Protector, and honour and venerate you in the face of Christ, according to the limited measure of our power, so that we pray to him, whose vicar we call you, thus: "not us, Lord, not us, but your name give the glory."[2] Hence we will proclaim in that light all those praiseworthy deeds which honour thee and justly so, for if you take upon yourself the responsibility both to amend, and to defend the wrongs which we and all your subjects have committed, then to you with justice also belongs the honour for all the good which we with God's help have accomplished.

Did not the good Teacher, whose vicar you are, call his disciples, standing apart or slow to believe in their hearts or some such thing,[3] and defend them before those who criticised them, drew the splinters from their own eyes and other similar things with the unconquerable might of his Spirit.[4] Thus inspired, I bring your Highness my humble work as an offering. Should corrections and improvements be necessary, edit with good counsel. But should envy speak ill words, then defend this work, as our Master did, for you are his faithful imitator and take his place. But if it is said that a work in need of correction is no offering for so venerable a lord, then we will respond thus: "We decry the poor rustic style, yet the work is valuable; the form may be despised, yet it is acceptable because of the merit of its contents." In order to acclaim the worth which—I promise—this story contains, I wrote of every deed with sober words and to the best of my ability: I wrote the life of the holy Mother Adelheid.

God counted her amongst his elected ones who interceded ceaselessly for his people. Through signs of power and wonders he has often manifested this. It will firstly profit you, and after you, all others faithful in Christ, to know by what good deeds she reached the heights of this holiness. May your wisdom decree that, recorded here by my pen or by some one else's, the memory of the subject discussed here will never pale and that all may hear the news of those unforgettable deeds performed with God's grace. But you must do your part, and give humble thanks to the Lord who through God became man, and lives as God and reigns with the Father in the unity of the Holy Spirit, the Paraclete, in all eternity. Amen.

CHAPTER TWO

Your wholesome example as well as your sweet motherly training, through which I have reached the present strength of my mind and age, without doubt demand of me, that I ascribe to you, venerable ladies and mothers, all the praise for that ability, even if I can exercise only a hint of learned discourse. So I believe, I must also thank you that I have accomplished now through divine largesse what I had vowed in spirit for a long time. Thus I have written of the life and virtue of the venerable virgin Saint Adelheid, because I deemed it an injustice that these should be covered with silence and thus could fall into oblivion.

Thus, that it should be secured through the strength of unconquerable truth, I have based my narrative partly upon the testimony of those of you whom the Mother, when she was still alive, taught both through instruction and example; and partly upon the testimony of that woman, the faithful servant woman,[5] namely Engilrada, who, as we know well, has outstripped you all in age and thus could remember more of the story and and better than any of you. She has revealed certain ancestral connections to royalty and many of the family's great honours.

After my humble pen had recorded all of this faithfully, this trustworthy witness ended the journey of her life. Herein one should recognise that the unfathomable depth of divine reason had allowed her to live such a long time so that through her presence such great virtue could be made known to all the world with clarity. My conscience be my witness, that in my ignorance, this work would never have been written.[6] Not to presume on my power, but rather in humble reverence have I submitted to him, so that, if later a devoted admirer should bring this life into the light with an elegant style, he would find a truthful record already written. So that your verdict of this work, which cannot support itself on the grace of fulsome words, would not condemn it on the basis of the lowness of my person, upon which in truth all look down, I decided to circulate it among some credible men who are sufficiently knowledgeable in the liberal arts.[7] These men have approved it after repeated reading and have declared it worthy to be seen by the public.

But before it is published, I flee for refuge to the shelter of your loving kindness, for I refuse no amendment, either from you or anyone else, as long as it is made with charity. In humility I beg you, though you may censor the form, which does not glitter with artful poetry, as well as my temerity, that at least you must approve the truth of the happenings herein described.

I also beg, though my sins are repulsive, that through the merit of this work and the intercession of your prayers I might find inclusion in your higher community of daughters of this holy Mother, though I be the lowliest maid.

CHAPTER THREE

Let us begin the work with an exhortation of the Holy Spirit who has effected all good things which have ever existed. So this work also should be finished through the support of his gifts, for therein lies the beginning and the end of all good. If we consider our insignificance and inexperience, then we tremble at the attempt to begin a great work. But if we look to the bounty of divine reward, then the fear disappears, for the Spirit blows where he wills as the Gospel testifies.[8] We have faith that he will fill this writing with his breath because of the merits of our Mother, the holy Lady Adelheid. The praise-worthy chain of her life we, her lowliest maids, are trying to describe here, and we pray, that the Holy Spirit may inflame the spark of intelligence which nature has given us. But for now it seems only just to us that we should honour her noble lineage of which her name reveals the origins. Then we would like to renew with our writings further edification to those living now and to those to come the memory of her holy deeds, so that we will admire God's power to his glory, to him about whom the Apostle says that all in all is made.[9]

Her father, the illustrious Count Megengoz, had a great reputation for wisdom, nobility, and wealth among the princes of his time, so that he was regarded as and called a king though without the estate and title of a ruler. Her mother Gerberga, also of the highest lineage, was daughter to Duke Godfrey, a great man in his time. The noble matron also had four brothers who were counted among the most important magnates. One of them who bore the name and honours of his father, sadly died without tasting the happiness of a beloved wife and children. Another was granted high noble descendants and was the ancestor of the recently deceased Emperor Henry III. All the illustrious magnates, through whom German Frankland is ennobled to this day, take their high rank from the other two brothers, as testimony bears out.

Megengoz and Gerberga strove in the light of their earthly glory to illuminate glowing virtues before the Lord, and thus their honour was augmented through the birth of a son. By tradition he was given the name of his grandfather Godfrey and by divine favour he was granted his powerful virtue and omen. They also had four daughters; two they gave in marriage in the hope that heirs would follow. Both became illustrious through the might of their husbands and the affluence of all their goods and riches. One of them, Irmentrud by name, was the grandmother of Henry, the illustrious duke, of Adalbero, bishop of Metz, of Duke Frederick, and of his brothesr, truly men of great lineage in our time. But the other, called Alvarada, was also the ancestress of a celebrated progeny.[10]

The remaining two daughters dedicated themselves in Cologne to divine service and law; one, Bertrada, in the convent of Mary Mother of God. She advanced so far in her moral striving and her observances of the Rule,[11] that justly she was granted the dignity of Lady and Mother of the convent. But Adelheid, about whom we are speaking here, took upon herself the sweet yoke of the Lord in the convent of the holy virgins after the rule established by St. Jerome.[12]

As an infant, she already presaged the tenderness which would later manifest itself as uprightness. Even before she had outgrown her girlhood, she began with devotion to engage herself in philosophical studies. After she recognised through her studies her rational soul she sought the refreshment of the salt of wisdom with steady labour. God, however, who gives to all in abundance, permitted it to happen without hesitation, for he foresaw that all this profusion would be of great use. Thus nourished, she began to grow so much in virtue and probity that she was far ahead of her young years in the gravity of her manners and had reached in habits and deeds that maturity which the Scriptures recommend in the words of the prophet: "For an honoured old age does not depend on length of time and is not measured by the number of one's years."[13]

Meanwhile her brother Godfrey who had grown up to be a man advanced wonderfully in virile strength, grace and quickness. He accompanied the emperor to Bohemia with the army, followed by the honourable soldiers of his well-armed levy. This brave and distinguished warrior won in battle a glorious death. After much travail, his followers carried his body back to his homeland with great honour, thanks be to God.

Following this stroke of ill fortune, his parents remembered that the Apostle said that the substance of the world would pass away,[14] and they began to conduct their relations with the world in such a way as if they had no need of it and strove for the heavenly home which they knew to be without end. Therefore, they made God the heir of the whole estate which, after a just partition, would have been the son's part, because since their son was surprised here in this vale of tears by an early death, he would be deprived of his inheritance, though he would gain a better one in heaven. Then they built a new church at a place called Vilich to the honour of God and enriched it suitably with landed estates and other possessions. And both, though still well and healthy, decided for the sake of Christ to end their conjugal habits although they were closely united, one heart and one soul, through their spiritual ties and their joint care about the work they had begun.

Megengoz served outwardly in the world because of the pressing demands of his own people and also of the strangers who came to honour him as to a king so that with Christ's help, he increased and protected his possessions and left all things prudently and justly in good order. But when he found that the people had dispersed for a while and he had some quiet and ease for himself, then he sought to fill these moments with worthy deeds. He called the chaplains and let them interpret the divine books in the German language. He desired this so fervently because he meant to turn the Apostle James' commandment into deeds who had said, "But be doers of the word, and not hearers only."[15]

Lady Gerberga, that noble matron, remote from the multitude, remained steadfastly at the place where the monastery was to be built, accelerating the pressing work on the structure with magisterial foresight. She was always intent on divine service, fasting and praying night and day. These actions were committed with such a faith that she clearly surpassed the widows who, after the death of their husbands, created virtue out of necessity and whom the Apostle himself praised for their continence.[16] Gerberga was not compelled to act thus through the death of her husband but because she was totally touched within herself by the flame of divine love.

Then they collected together a community of virgins in that place who were to tend the divine service. From the convent of the Holy Virgins, they redeemed their daughter with a gift of land, and handed over to her the care of the future direction and government of Vilich. Thus constituted as prudent stewardess in the house of the great heavenly

Father, Adelheid began to make a greater effort in all study
and good works, exhibiting a motherly care for those under
her and faithfully paying out to each their portions at the
proper time.[17] Then the pious parents exulted in the Lord as
they saw their offspring and her virgin subordinates and
longing for them to lay hold of the higher way, they begged
Adelheid that she should change her dress and begin a life of
monastic conversion.[18] Adelheid however, still young, much
desired the adorned dress accorded to her religious rank as
canoness. And she herself asserted this willingly to her
parents and in humble response withstood their petition:
God did not desire *forced* service but a willing and guileless
heart presented in purity. Her parents paid attention to her
humble responses and withheld their wishes, well aware of
her religious calling.

When they had decorated the place worthily, they gave it
into the hand of the Emperor Otto III, so that his protection
would defend it in perpetuity. Graciously he freed the place
from all secular yoke and laws and bestowed upon it the liber-
ties according to the laws and constitutions of the convents
of Gandersheim, Quedlinburg and Essen, namely that a judge
or advocate could never demand services thereupon nor
could govern in the boundaries of the area of that convent
unless it pleased the abbess and her congregation. Also the
sisters should possess the power to elect their abbess in their
holy association in perpetuity. In order that this donation of
freedom be established firmly, it was confirmed with manuscripts and seals by a bull of the pope and two charters by the
emperors, Otto III and Henry II. Today these are preserved
faithfully in our custody so that the truth will not be hidden
from posterity.

Not long thereafter the Lord called home into his realm the Lady Gerberga, freed of all earthly cares. Upon her coming, he found her vigilant and faithfully persevering in her Catholic faith and in her good works: without doubt she was granted as recompense those blessings which the Lord promised to the watchful servant in the Gospels.

Thus deprived of the help of her mother, the noble off-spring turned ardently to God whom she had loved as a child. Touched through God's omnipotent grace with a wholesome regret, she now placed before the eyes of her mind the change of habit which she had strongly gainsaid to her parents. She considered at all moments how she might finally become fulfilled through the monastic principles.[19] Wisdom forbade to begin that change suddenly and advised her to consider the necessary strengths in the quietness of her mind, whether they be sufficient to take on the Rule of St. Benedict, so that should they be broken, she would not come under the reprimand of the Gospel word: "This man began to build, and was not able to finish it."[20]

Thus she held in contempt the daily hour of restoration, the meat and other food which was well selected and varied and was content only with monastic foods. This she did, however, without the knowledge of her table companions, except one good sister, who was a silent accomplice. In public she shone in linen garments but next to her skin she wore a rough woollen garment in the spirit of repentance and thus she subdued the soft nature of her noble body so that she might suffer the dictates of a hard law for the sake of God. When, after a year, she had summoned up the necessary strength and hoped that it would be sufficient to continue the work she had begun, Adelheid put into action the long delib-erated silent vow, not alone, but with the grace of God. Then she called upon the venerable abbess and the leaders of the Cologne convent of the Holy Mother of God and humbly put herself under their knowledgeable guidance so that through their teachings she would find the way into the order.

In motherly piety she gave the sisters under her the advice that they should not hesitate to go this way with her. When some did not wish to do so but instead returned back into the world, she was deeply pained for, with the Apostle, she wished that all would be like her.[21]

To those, however, who were strengthened by the love of God and of her and who did not leave the convent, she showed herself a shining example in the way of salvation, so that she, who outranked all in dignity and office, submitted herself more than all the others to the demands of the Rule and, through fasting and praying, tried to sustain the others in such a manner that none would falter. In her zeal for the right she began to censor all backsliding so that the holy life would not be cut down in its first growth. In her heart she was a loving mother but she practised outward severity. She used the rod on the flesh so that the soul would be saved at the day of the Lord. She took care that the zeal for rectitude was tempered by the spirit of clemency, for her maternal nature felt that justice became severity when it exceeded moderation.[22]

After she had given a punishment, like a mother, she was touched by a compassionate clemency and spoke to the older sisters who through their order and their good behaviour merited such trust: "O how miserable I am about my daughters that I had to inflict such grave punishment; thus I pray and warn you, speak to them lovingly with merciful consolations and admonitions so that they do not sink into sadness, but turn from their wickedness and turn to God and to me in filial love."

O what loving and benign words, worthy to be held forever in memory! Thus she mixed at times caresses with strong terror, after the command of the Apostle[23] and she continued her reproaches, blandishments and prayers until she had rid their troublesome souls of the vicious pest.

CHAPTER FOUR

Lord Megengoz lived for three years after the death of his wife. Fulfilled in every goodness by the grace of the Holy Spirit, a wise and just leader, he strove towards heavenly virtue. When God called him, he departed from this world in a place called Geldern, not doubting that he would receive the crown from him, to whom he had devoted himself zealously. On the very night of his death, as his holy daughter lay on her bed in repose, neither fully awake nor yet asleep—or so she asserted—someone seemed to stand by her and sweetly sang the words of the prophet into her ear: "See, the righteous man perishes, and no one can lays it to heart. The devout men are taken away, etc."[24] She told the sisters of this vision early the next morning and when she had completed her story, a messenger came and brought the news that Megengoz had departed this world. His daughter had him brought for burial to her own convent where he was interred in a place of honour next to his wife with all proper religious ceremony. Later, he appeared in a dream to one of the sisters of the convent, clothed in all the power and glory of regal majesty. After she had looked at him for a while and hesitantly asked him whether he was the Lord Megengoz, he gave her this joyful answer: "That was once my name when I still bore the weight of the body. Now I am truly called Megengaudus, a better name, for, free from the fetters of sin, I enjoy eternal bliss, united with all the saints and patriarchs in heaven."

Since the holy virgin enjoyed full rights over all her possessions after the death of her father, she took good care that
nothing would obstruct those on the right way. And remembering the precepts of the holy father, St. Benedict, through
her deeds, she acquired the name and status of a mother who
gave to those in need without thought of recompense. In the
winter when, after early matins, they went back to their
dormitories, Adelheid herself checked the girls' beds and
rubbed their feet with her loving hands until they were warm
again. Contrary to the Rule, she did not leave the care of sick
sisters to other prudent and careful sisters but she herself
attended to them every day without interference. She would
humbly kneel before the bed of each sister and gently holding their heads up in her hands, she would lovingly give them
food and drink and tears would fall down her noble cheeks as
if she herself had borne them from her womb. Thus with such
a shepherd watching over them, the sheep were freed from
worldly cares and made such great advances in the life of the
Rule that soon they became an example of virtue to the
founders of their spiritual principles.

CHAPTER FIVE

Once Adelheid had settled all interior matters satisfactorily
with God's help, she was impelled to turn her attention to the
outside world for she also desired to serve the kingdom of God
there. Filled thus with faith and hope for the greater reward
which the Lord promised when he said, "Seek ye first the kingdom, and all else will be granted unto you,"[25] she set aside one
manor from the possessions of the convent to the Lord
alone.[26] Fifteen paupers were to be fed and clothed for all eter-

nity from its annual returns and harvests by her mandate and
every Christmas these beggars were to be given fifteen *solidi* of
money as well. Another fifteen beggars she had looked after by
the convent who were to receive annually a fixed sum at Lent,
twelve *solidi* at the feast days of each Apostle throughout the
year, and on at least three of the quarter-days[27] they were to
receive the full measure of payment in kind. She frequently
ordered the sisters to assent to these regulations unanimously
and they were not allowed the dissolution of the regulations
under her successors. Adelheid predicted truthfully that if
anyone decreased these donations, they would jeopardise their
happiness in the hereafter as well as in the present. I have
reported this so that the donations would not be forgotten and
hence be observed for all eternity.

CHAPTER SIX

At one time, almost the whole world was afflicted by a bitter
famine and great masses of the starving came from everywhere, to partake of her generosity, as from the breast of a
mother.[28] All through the streets and at every crossroad many
lay half-dead and waited for the accustomed dispensing of
her alms. Touched by their great need, Adelheid herself cared
with devotion for every one. To the healthy and robust she
parcelled out bread and bacon; the ill she served cabbage and
vegetables carefully boiled with meat. The dying and those
almost despairing of life she revived with broths mixed with
water and flour and other nourishment, always watching
with diligence that the body not be put in peril by overeating
after a lack of proper food.

She lit this light of her good heart before men to the glory
of her Father in heaven. Often her left hand did not acknowl-

edge what her right hand was doing. She was always ready to give alms even in secret and if she did not have money on hand when the poor called upon her, she stealthily took off her shoes and put them in the beggar's vessel. Only the heavenly Father witnessed these acts and she took care lest other people's eyes should observe them. Should we try to touch all this in detail, our narrative would never come to an end, for thus the Lord made manifest in her his word, when he said, "For to every one who has will more be given, and he will have abundance."[29] Holding God and her neighbours in high regard, she received great love from everyone so that she was strengthened with the external benefits of earthly riches and with the internal gift of spiritual virtue.

Thus Adelheid aided and strengthened the institutions of religious ceremonies and the schools of divine service which were always the most important responsiblities of her office. Adelheid would visit them frequently and ask questions on grammar and when she received a correct answer, she would reward the pupil quickly with a maternal kiss, filled as she was with spiritual joy at the prospect of further advances. O Love, admired by all who heard of it, great, tenacious, and ceaseless, always glowing for the good, which never—God be thanked— gave way to evil.

During this time, her aforementioned sister Bertrada died blessedly in Christ. The Archbishop, St. Heribert, well aware that our Mother was richly endowed with all virtues, wished that she follow her sister in the governance of the convent. Adelheid, however, protested with all her might and said that she was not worthy to carry so great an honour. The emperor, who was at that time in Aachen, was soon told that Adelheid would yield her consent neither to the command nor to the prayers of the bishop. The emperor called her to his court and by his command, he raised her to the office of her deceased sister.

Through the Lord's will, word of Adelheid's accomplishments at Vilich reached the capital city of Cologne. According to the judgement of the archbishop, no one in the whole order was her equal in wisdom, piety and sanctity. For that reason the venerable high priest held her in such esteem that he always followed her advice in spiritual matters. Between these two was such a wonderful love and God-willed trust that in all good deeds they seemed to be of one mind. That is why, without doubt, they are now united in heaven in the same eternal home. O happy Cologne of those days, administered according to divine law by that eager imitator of Peter, teacher and leader of the entire people and clergy, and by that saintly woman, so remarkable, so great and religious, leading the choir of virgins. For this venerable abbess, lady and mother of virgins, whom the heavenly Father had put in charge of the many, after she had been faithful over the few,[30] watched carefully and diligently over her double herd, following the example of the good Shepherd. At all times she repeated in her secret heart the words of the Gospel, "Everyone to whom much is given, of him will much be required."[31]

To those, however, whom she had born in the Lord in Vilich and had nourished with the pure milk of wholesome doctrine,[32] she especially imparted with her maternal love. It should come as no surprise to anyone that what is more dearly obtained is more dearly possessed. All the glorious splendour of Cologne could never separate her from her memories and it always pained her to go away for a long time when in spirit she longed to be at her accustomed place. But if the daughters were granted the return of their mother, they cried for such joy as if they had seen God himself. Like the hen which gathers her chicks under her wings, thus did Adelheid draw them all to her in wondrous love and kindness. She would look at each one—their appearance, their dress, their well-being—and would carefully inquire whether they had suffered any loss in her absence. She was truly a good shepherd, not a hired servant, for she could never endure that her own should miss the necessities of life. Without the knowledge of the cellaress or other sisters she often went secretly into the store rooms and took wine, meat, fish and much other good food which she distributed to the younger sisters. And for this memorable theft she herself would replace anything that was missing from the exact measure of the provisions.

CHAPTER SEVEN

She decided to do this thing in secret[33] because she sought a reward from the heavenly Father who sees in secret and because she was often chastised by her charges for her lavish generosity. O thus does deceit which is praised, not without merit, and which is remembered now and forever as right although considered a great crime by human judgement, become a wondrous virtue through the actions of maternal love. Although these acts would lead to punishment for many, she, on the other hand, will gain virtue and heavenly acclaim. O precious jewel of virgins who so displayed all the splendours of virtue before that great and glorious God that the Lord made manifest his miraculous ways, transforming her during this earthly peregrination.

If, for instance, it happened that one of the sisters could not keep the harmony of the choir of loudly singing voices (for is it not written that "none of us can do everything"?[34]) and the good mother would correct her and box her ears, then for the rest of her life the sister had a beautiful voice and

sang clearly. In the same manner she often reproached some
sisters who suffered from long-term illnesses that they were
wasting their time uselessly if they did not labour with their
hands and shortly after she had reproached them, they were
healed by the grace of the Lord. Once Adelheid sent an urgent
message to the cellaress just as she was extracting wine from
the casket. The cellaress obediently followed the command
but she forgot to close the hole of the casket and when she
presented herself before the abbess without delay, she was
still carrying the stop of the casket in her hand. When she
realised what had happened, she was unduly apprehensive
concerning the spilled wine. The holy abbess comforted her
with maternal kindness and spoke these gentle words: "O
sister, I do not wish to see you so sad over this mishap, for the
damage can be repaired through the power and grace of God.
Nevertheless, let us go and see what has happened and give
thanks to God, be it good or bad." When they entered the
cellar, both equally concerned, they saw that not a drop of
wine had flowed out or had been spilled, the cellaress threw
herself at the feet of the mother and attributed the miracle to
her sanctity. But Adelheid instead said, that according to
divine power, it was more the result of the cellaress' obedience and she forbade her to divulge the incident as long as
she lived. The cellaress, however, thought it unjust to conceal
that sign of divine power and, in praise of God, she made it
known secretly to certain other sisters. In this and all other
matters which the Lord wrought through her hands, Adelheid
always retreated from the exaltation of worldly acclaim,
recalling that it was too dangerous to praise the happiness of
those still navigating the great and wide sea of life, for her
soul continually doubted that she would reach the refuge of
the desired harbour.[35] But our Father in heaven, the knowl-

edgeable approver and witness of every deed performed in secret, did not wish that this light be hidden under a bushel,[36] but rather it be placed upon a candelabra and light up for many the splendour of his goodness. Still brighter did she illuminate the world after the Lord had led her, freed of doubts, to safe harbour after her voyage over the sea [of life].

Now the Lord, who according to the Scriptures gives to everyone his due,[37] decided to reward her for all her good deeds and she slowly lost her physical strength. She, however, continued in her standards of virtue since, as the voice of the Lord said to the Apostle: " . . . for my power is made perfect in weakness."[38] As the day of her death drew near, she was visiting the convent of Santa Maria the Mother of God (Santa Maria-im-Kapitol at Cologne) to fulfill her administerial duties. On the evening of the feast day of St. Blaise[39] right after the evening meal, she was struck with a terrible pain in her throat. After the singing of the compline and as she was reclining on her small bed, she revealed her sickness to one Ida, a sister she had raised in her own convent according to the Rule and who was wont to accompany her on her journeys.

Ida, hoping that the illness was not serious, returned to her own warm bed but Adelheid, certain that this pain was her death, remained awake throughout the night in fear of death which both the just and the wicked must suffer for it is a bitter and strong fear. But no one should wonder at this, for even the Lord himself fell into anguish at his approaching death.

She could not endure the length of the night stretched out on her bed and therefore she sought the sanctuary and heard the matins sung and thus did she persist in the service of God with all her remaining strength. At the first dawning of the new day, she had celebrated for herself the sacrament of the Mass, and was fortified by the body and blood of our Lord.

Then she requested St. Heribert to come and see her and her
people. When he was assured of her approaching death from
what she said, he was shaken beyond all measure in his heart
that in her death he would be separated from her to whom in
life he was allied with indissoluble love. Nevertheless she held
firmly to her responsibilities towards her charges in Vilich
until the end and informed them through a special messenger that she was a little ill and asked that they should come
with all possible haste in order to see her. But alas, not realis-
ing the coming misery, they decided to delay the journey
until the following day. Meanwhile her holy soul, dissolved
from the ties of the flesh, entered rejoicing into paradise to
which she had ceaselessly aspired in life and there to be eter-
nally with Christ. When the messenger came to Vilich to tell
the sisters of her death, their sorrow was very great; it is still
painful to be reminded of it. One would rather weep than to
report any more of their misery and unhappiness.

The sisters believed that the best remedy for their sorrow
would be to allow the deceased to be interred in her hered-
itary cloister. Therefore they presented themselves to the
bishop, threw themselves at his feet, and begged him with
tears that he would mercifully permit the body to rest with
those from whom in life she had never wished to be separated. The archbishop foresaw in the Holy Spirit what God
had planned to do through her in the future and for a time
he remained inexorable and hard but later, conquered by
their pleas and mindful of God's warnings, he was moved to
pity and gave them the body which they had requested with
many tears so that they could lay it in its final resting place.
He spoke to them, himself in tears: "If I had the high favour
and owned the body of Virgin Agatha, whose feast day the
Church is celebrating today, as God is my witness, I would

not differentiate between this one and that, for without doubt her beautiful soul is precious to God."

Now that the sisters of Vilich had received permission to take the body there, the worthy bishop, with all men and women of the monastic community and the entire population of the city, followed after her in a large crowd. And as soon as the sacred body was placed with all religious honours upon the ship and even before the oars were in place, the vessel sailed quickly upstream against the current without the aid of the rowers. The people of Cologne realised through this display of divine power that to deprive Adelheid's daughters in Vilich of the sacred body was not God's will.

Now when the funeral rites[40] had been properly celebrated, and when, without doubt, her soul exalted in the fields of paradise, the daughter of Adelheid's own sister, whom she herself had educated, succeeded in her place of honour according to the will of God. She possessed great moral strength, an elegant face and figure—surely evidence of the excellence of her noble descent.

CHAPTER EIGHT

Now that we have told all the above, we want to make known the miraculous signs which the Lord made known to the world through her manifest virtues, fulfilling the duty of praise to him whose favour she had earned.

Before the thirtieth day after her death when the poor flocked into the monastic cloisters in order to receive their alms, a blind man came to that place so that he be shown the glory of divine virtue. Through the negligence of his guide he inadvertently hit his head against the tombstone, and fell to the ground. But presently through her goodness he arose

again, his vision restored. As a result of this event, desolation
and grief were forgotten and in all our rooms there arose a
song of delight. Yet soon greater joy followed this delight and
all the doubt which had oppressed some hearts went away
completely at this first sign.

CHAPTER NINE

A woman was greatly bothered by an ulcer on her shin and
could move only with difficulty, supported by a walking-
stick. Alerted by a vision she decided to come to the tomb
where, through her [i.e. Adelheid's] intervention, she was
healed. When she publicly announced the good result to the
praise of God in that place, another woman disparaged the
occurrence by saying that she had been lying. Not long after,
the accuser was possessed by the devil but before the evil one
departed, exhorted and bound with many divine words, he
acknowledged the wonders which Christ had already done
and would continue to do through his virgin. And when the
woman was dragged to the site of the tomb, he departed the
possessed soul with a great deal of vomit.

As the news of this and more signs and divine favours were
spread abroad, the number of people gathering from the far
corners of the world was as great as those living nearby.
Though the cloister was by no means small, the proper quiet
for the regular observances of the religious life of the sisters
was much disturbed—more than seemed decent.

Remembering the precept of the Lord that the man invited
to a wedding should seek the last place to recline at table, the
highly blessed Lady, when she was still alive, had herself
requested that she not be buried in a sacred place but in the
cloister when she would depart this world, following God's

call. But the Lord acknowledged the humility of his maid-servant[41] and he who rules with such great dominion over all his creatures, spoke also to her, "Friend, go up higher, and you will be honoured."[42] And God himself saw to it that the Lady, transferred in all honours within the walls of the minster, was there commemorated with the other saints to all eternity.

CHAPTER TEN

As henceforth in more and more places the fame of the signs grew, everyone who was plagued by an illness or another trouble swiftly came to that place, certain that they would be healed, the number of those assembling at her tomb knew no end.

Among them also came a nobleman who by a papal decree was chained in iron for penance of a crime. After he had wandered to the thresholds of many sanctuaries, he was finally freed through her [i.e. Adelheid's] manifest grace and the sound of the disintegrating and widely scattered chains was heard by all who were then in the convent. With great humanity the venerable Abbess, truly endowed with the kindness of her maternal aunt, took in the absolved one for a long time, as well as his full brother who loved his brother as himself and who, though innocent, had taken up the chains and shared all the labours with him, and had made amends for the offenses of his brother. After the numbed arms and legs had gradually been revitalised to their former strength through the alleviating treatment of such kindness, the Abbess helped them with clothes and horses and allowed them to return home, joyful in their hearts. Also on the feast day of the Chains of St. Peter [August 1], who is our special patron and to whose honour this monastery is dedicated, a lame man, deprived of his hearing and his sight, received the gift of health at the tomb of the sacred Virgin.

CHAPTER ELEVEN

If a peasant brought a gift, not from among his abundant possessions but, of his free will, to show her his pure intentions, then he would win an increase in all that he needed through her faithful intervention. So that there be no doubt, we faithfully relate the case of one poor woman to whom the faithful recompensor appeared in a nightly dream. She [i.e. Adelheid] issued the powerful command, that the poor woman should present her with a white dress of her own making. But when she answered that she could not satisfy this request because she was too poor, she strongly urged her to arise at dawn and petition her neighbours in her name for the missing items. At the break of day and without delay, she requested of her fellow citizens those things she needed to comply with the command of the holy virgin and she received so much linen that not only did she make the alb but a much needed dress for herself as well. After she had placed the alb at the sepulchre, she received so many gifts that for the rest of her life, at the anniversary of that date, she made a donation of an ox or some such thing.

These and other innumerable miracles through which the Lord at that time caused her to shine in splendour are so many that our insignificant pen cannot set them down one by one. A few of these miracles which happened in our time and which [I]we heard ourselves and saw with our own eyes, however, we should not pass over be held in contempt for our silence.

CHAPTER TWELVE

One night the only son of a woman, eight years old and so infirm since birth that all his limbs were incapable of use except for his tongue and eyes, saw as in a dream that the holy virgin stood by his bed and released all the nervous cramps and contractions. When he began to cry with great shouts because of the loosening of his limbs, everyone in the house was jolted from their sleep and came near his bed. They discovered him almost lifeless, but with his limbs in natural position and form. After an hour's time he regained consciousness and made known to all around him what he had dreamed and he urged his father and mother to take him immediately to the tomb of the holy virgin with a gift.

In the joy of their son's healing they prepared the gift without delay. Putting the boy on a horse, they themselves set off on foot for the journey. Then God, who acts in truly wonderful ways through his saints, permitted to occur a piteously miserable event, so that they, when saved from it, would see his work even more wonderful. For when they crossed the bridge over the river, the horse carrying the boy leaped from the bridge and immersed itself and the boy in the water and disappeared for almost an hour. When the parents cursed from their hearts at the seeming loss of their son and cried out that holy Adelheid was impious and cruel and undeserving of her place with God, they suddenly saw the horse coming to the bank with the child on its back. Then their tears were turned to cries of joy and laughter and they continued their journey and came to Vilich on the feast day of St. Gereon [October 10], when the first bell sounded the office of matins.

CHAPTER THIRTEEN

Yet another man was freed from the devil's possession who, as long as he lived, annually brought a gift to her tomb in recompense for his sanity.

What more can be said! God gave Adelheid in this world all the signs and virtues through which, except for the resurrection, he revealed his infinite wisdom. Praise and glory be to him, world without end. Amen.

2 A Century of Women: German Aristocratic Families in the Tenth- & Eleventh Centuries

THE *VITA ADELHEIDIS ABBATISSAE VILICENSIS AUCTORE BERTHA* IS AN historical biography of thirteen chapters written in an elegant rhymed prose by the nun Bertha, a composition which has a genuine place of honour among the surviving Latin works from the eleventh century.[43] Indeed, if the *Vita Adelheidis* were regarded merely as a short life of the Abbess Adelheid, a glimpse at her convent and the lives of her nuns and canonesses, the Latin text and now, hopefully, the English translation, would be a valuable source for it provides insights into the affairs and events of a community of women.

But the importance of the *Vita Adelheidis* goes far beyond that immediate appeal. In its opening chapters it presents a complicated family history which has been recognised as a major source for a complex series of events occurring in the early eleventh century: the so-called Hammersteiner divorce.[44]

Scholarly research into this divorce uncovered the problematic relationship of Otto and Irmingard of Hammerstein,
linking them both to a network of aristocratic families which
in some degree was connected to the Vilich abbey.[45]

Even a cursory glance at the primary sources of the tenth
and eleventh centuries shows clearly that the political and
social actions and decisions therein described originate with
a group of families allied in all sorts of ways to the royal house.
It was not, however, only the men from these families who
were important; their wives, mothers, sisters and daughters
were also present in the centers of power. Thus Helmut
Diwald in his biography of Henry ꞏI, the founder of the
Saxon/Ottonian dynasty, comments:

> Als besonders wichtiges Merkmal erscheint in diesem
> Zusammenhang die selbstbewußte Stellung der Frau in
> der Gesellschaft, die Sicherheit und Kraft ihrer Präsen-
> tation. Der Unterschied gegenüber späteren Zeiten ist
> so auffallig, daß man das zehnte Jahrhundert in
> Deutschland geradezu als das Jahrhundert der Frauen
> bezeichneten darf.[46]

The story of Vilich as told by Bertha can be said to be one
of those literary sources that provide the basis for Diwald's
opinion. It is a book about a woman, a community of women,
and it was written by a woman. It is also a book deeply
concerned with family and the sacrifices families make in order
to provide what they deem best for all the members. Vilich
owed its origin to two pious and grieving parents, Megengoz
and Gerberga. It is their story with which Bertha began and it
is indeed fittng to follow her lead.

Gerberga is central to that story. She was born c. 925/30 in Lotharingia, the daughter of a Count Palatine called Godfrey[47] and his wife Ermentrud. She also had four brothers, one named after his father, died young;[48] another was probably the great-grandfather of the Emperor Henry III.[49] What is also important about Gerberga is her name: it is one of the female names that occurs frequently among the Saxon/Ottonian royal family. That fact alone can give an informed family historian a clue to a possible family connection. Fortunately, the *Vita Adelheidis* is not the only source for the family of the Vilich founders. Gerberga's connection with the Ottonians can also be traced through a genealogy appended to the canons of a synod, held in Seligenstadt in 1023 by Aribo Archbishop of Mainz.[50] Appraisal of that genealogy suggests that her father Godfrey, son of one Gozlin and his wife Uda, had as his maternal grand-parents Oda, sister of Henry I of Germany, and her second husband Gerhard (†910), a noble of Lotharingia.[51] As well, at the time of Gerberga's birth, c. 930, Lotharingia was ruled by Giselbert, husband to Henry I's daughter Gerberga, and the niece of our Gerberga's grandmother. Widowed in 939, the duchess Gerberga then married Louis IV *Outremer* of France, and her association with the Lotharingian aristocracy contin-ued to be a close one; Megengoz, Gerberga's husband, was certainly a prominent member of that group. He was a native of Geldern; the couple lived on his lands there after their marriage and raised their family there. Born c. 920, the young man had become involved in the troubles in Lotharingia in 938 and 939, when Henry, then duke of Lotharingia, revolted against the authority of his brother, King Otto I of Germany. For this perhaps youthful mistake, Megengoz was deprived of his lands but in 944 he was pardoned by the king and a charter survives in the records of Vilich which returned his lands to him.[52] Whether or not he was already married is not known. Gerberga would have been old enough for marriage in 944; given the estimated ages of their children, the couple was certainly married by 950.[53] They had one son and four daughters. The son Godfrey, born c. 950/955, was killed in 977 while fighting with Otto II at the Slavic frontier. Of the daughters, Bertrada, abbess of Santa Maria-im-Kapitol in Cologne, seems to have been the eldest: born c. 950, she died c. 1000. Irmintrud or Imiza, married to Count Heribert of the Wetterau, was born c. 952, this date having been established in relationship to the probable births of her children. Gebhard, the eldest, was born about 970 and died 1016 without issue and certainly as an adult, having succeeded his father in 992 as count.[54] Gerberga[55] was born about 972, married Frederick of Luxemburg and produced four sons, all of whom were influential in the 1040's and 1050's and died well into the eleventh century. The younger Gerberga's marriage may have taken place about 995, about the time of Irmintrud's death. The youngest son was Otto of Hammerstein who inherited the county and the family wealth from his brother in 1016 and who was then married to Irmingard, daughter of Godfrey of Verdun. Megengoz and Gerberga's third daughter Alverada was born no later than 960. She married, but little is known about her husband or children other than the fact that if Adelheid was succeeded as abbess in Vilich by her niece, she would probably have been Alverada's daughter. Alverada's descendants could also have been the family of the counts of Jülich who were the lay advocates of Vilich in the twelfth century.[56]

The provisions which Gerberga made for the Vilich abbey, contained in the 987 charter and recounted in the *vita*, portray a dedicated mother who had provided for all her family, including the dead warrior-son, to the best of her ability and within the confines of her belief system. To this end she separated from her husband, with his consent, and set about her task with the help of her youngest daughter Adelheid.[57] Gerberga died about 995. Her activities as foundress of an abbey followed a pattern set by other members of her wider family circle. Queen Mathilde of Germany's foundation at Quedlinburg can be cited as an example; the strong leadership asserted by another Gerberga, the niece of Otto I, in her position as abbess of Gandersheim could also be seen as a model.

Indeed, some of the most influential women in the story of Vilich are those members of the Saxon/Ottonian royal family who dominate the history of the tenth century. Three strong central characters are particularly important: Mathilda, wife of Henry I; Adelheid, wife of Otto I; and Theophanu, wife of Otto II—in other words mother, daughter-in-law, and granddaughter-in-law. Each of these women influenced a circle of others: there was also considerable conflict between them: one might say that the one characteristic these three queens shared was their distrust of the influence of the others.

Mathilda, who died in 968, was a descendent of the well-known eighth-century chieftain Widukind who had fought the take-over of Saxony by Charlemagne and his Franks for over thirty years. She married Henry Duke of Saxony about 910 and they produced five children. Henry became king of Germany in 919 and died in 936. He was succeeded by the eldest child of that marriage, his son Otto I, much to the chagrin of the second son, Henry, who had also sought the crown, possibly with the help of his mother Mathilda. Henry's defeat, his eventual reconciliation with his brother and his appointment to the duchy of

Bavaria also eased Otto's relationship with his mother. However, Mathilda remained a formidable matriarch, reluctant to share her power in the family circle, particularly with her daughter-in-law Adelheid, Otto's second wife, whom she considered a foreign interloper. Mathilda retired eventually to her own foundation, the abbey of Quedlinburg and her strongest influence was probably upon her granddaughters, her name sake Mathilda, daughter of Adelheid and Otto, who followed her in the administration of Quedlinburg, and Gerberga abbess of Gandersheim, daughter of Henry of Bavaria.[58]

The Empress Adelheid was more cosmopolitan in her origins and influence. Born in Burgundy c. 931 and married to the young king of Lombardy in her teens, she was a widow by 950 and imprisoned by her husband's successor. Her dramatic rescue and subsequent marriage to Otto I is the stuff of legends. Her close links with the abbey of Cluny made her the centre of a very wide circle of influential people and Abbot Odilo of Cluny (†1047) wrote her biography shortly after her death.[59] She was *consor regni* to Otto I not only in name; in her widowhood her influence at first retreated before the power of her daughter-in-law, Theophanu, but was stronger than ever when, upon Theophanu's death in 991, Adelheid became regent for Otto III.[60]

The Empress Theophanu undoubtedly was most directly involved with Vilich and its inmates. Not only was the foundation charter drawn up under her guidance, but members of the Vilich founding family were among her closest associates; eventually one of her granddaughters became abbess of Vilich.

Theophanu has long been one of the most problematic members of the Ottonian royal family. Otto I had been determined that his son and heir Otto II was to marry the most suitable bride possible and that meant only one choice: a Princess *porphyrogenita* of the imperial house of Byzantium. To this end he had sent an embassy under his friend, Bishop Liutprand of Cremona, to Constantinople.[61] Although we have that worthy's description of his many adventures in this diplomatic quest, the end results of his mission have been as perplexing to historians as they were to the German imperial court. The princess originally designated refused to go or was not sent. The bride who came to Rome in 971 was most certainly Byzantine, even well-brought up, young, beautiful and elegant, but neither her new bridegroom nor her father-in-law were ever totally sure just who she was. Otto was advised to send her back, but his son, young and impetuous, had fallen in love, and Otto I probably felt that one Byzantine princess was as good as another. The German emperor must have felt that a bird in hand was better than a dove in the bush: he was not at all sure he would ever get another bride out of Constantinople. Theophanu's origins have been hotly debated ever since. She was called a niece of the general John Tzimisces who had just come to power in Constantinople, but whether she was a member of his family (he was Armenia) or perhaps a relation of his first wife, or whether she was a minor Macedonian and a member of his second wife's family and thus "of the purple born," has never come to light in a direct reference in a primary source.[62] Whatever the truth of the matter, Theophanu proved to be worthy of the love and trust her new family bestowed upon her. First as a loving wife to Otto II and mother of four children, and later as Dowager (983–991) when the regency for her infant son fell on her shoulders, Theophanu acted with great courage and great ability. In the decade that she was at the helm of the German

Miles

0 200

SAXONY

SLAVS

LORRAINE

FRANCONIA

BOHEMIA

SWABIA

BAVARIA

CARINTHIA

ITALY

Germany and Italy at the Time of Otto the Great

962

Germany at the Time of Otto the Great
962

Empire, few incidents escaped her immediate attention. This
included wars on the Slavic frontier, a major upheaval in
Italy, a disputed crown in France, or such a relatively minor
event as the founding of Vilich.[63]

We do not really know why Theophanu came to be so
closely linked with the Vilich foundation. It was certainly not
unusual for members of the royal family to endow convents,
but this endowment was rather different. Neither the
founders nor the land came from the immediate royal family;
all that was really "imperial" in the Vilich charter was the
granting of immunities from episcopal control, as was the
case for such major abbeys as Gandersheim and Quedlinburg.
But Theophanu may have had a personal reason to favour the
Vilich founding family, for she had a close association with
Irmintrud or Domna Imiza, the daughter of Gerberga and the
sister of the Abbess Adelheid.

In 983 Gerbert of Aurillac, the future pope Sylvester II
(999–1003) mentioned *Domna* Imiza in a letter he wrote to
Pope John IV.[64] On 20 March 984, after he had returned to
Rheims to serve as secretary and confidant to Archbishop Adalbero, Gerbert wrote the lady himself. He concluded his letter:

> Approach my Lady Theophanu in my name to inform
> her that the kings of the French are well disposed
> towards her son [Otto III], and that she should
> attempt nothing but the destruction of Henry's tyran-
> nical scheme, for he desires to make himself king
> under the pretext of guardianship."[65]

Imiza's role in the stirring events of 984 is not detailed, but
she must have returned with her mistress from Rome to
Germany. Indeed, her role at court is an interesting one, for
by the time Gerbert's letters were written, Imiza was married

and had three children, of whom Otto von Hammerstein, who was born c. 975, was probably the youngest. Her husband, Heribert Count of the Wetterau, may have been a member of the old ducal family of Franconia, but he could not be described as a "courtier." Whether Imiza also accompanied her royal friend to the *Colloquium dominarum*[66] in Metz in 985 is not known. She died about 995, probably at Vilich where she had gone in her widowhood.

Theophanu herself died in her mid-thirties on 15 June, 991. She was much mourned and her contemporaries praised her wise rule; her influence stretched from the Elbe frontier to Paris in the north and to Rome in the south. The events of her reign can be read in the histories of her day, and the diplomatic and legal output of her regency can be found in many archives. Her tomb is in the Church of St. Pantaleon in Cologne where a modern sarcophagus of Greek marble houses her remains and where worshippers say their prayers to this day.[67]

Another royal lady in the story of Vilich is Kunigunde, the wife of Henry II. The daughter of Siegfried of Luxemburg, she was born about 970 into a family of numerous brothers of singularly warlike and quarrelsome personalities. Kunigunde married Henry, then duke of Bavaria, at Easter in 1000 when he was twenty-seven and she nearly thirty. Kunigunde was very influential in her husband's reign; frequently she performed tasks which the pressure of time and other business prevented the king from undertaking. Yet her life was no bed of roses. Henry was often ill and could be very bad-tempered. The couple had no children—either by design or by accident—and the legend arose that their marriage was chaste, a claim which should be regarded with caution as there is some evidence against it in the sources.[68] On 14 February, 1014 Henry and Kunigunde received the imperial crowns in Rome from the Pope. In 1017 Kunigunde became very ill and she vowed that if she survived, she would build a convent. This she did at Kaufungen in 1018. Her closeness to her family, particularly to her brothers, caused her husband much trouble, but the frequent mention of her in the sources reveal that Kunigunde was an important member of Henry's government. She died in 1033, nine years after her husband and she was eventually canonised.[69] Her name is indelibly linked with Bamberg which was at first her dower land and which she returned to Henry when he wanted to create a new bishopric there. She is buried with her husband in an elaborate tomb, created by Tilman Riemenschneider c. 1500. A seventeenth-century statue of her graces the bridge over the Pregnitz.[70]

Kunigunde's association with Vilich is well-documented. In the 1003 charter reaffirming Vilich's immunities, Henry II declared that she was the intercessor and that it was at her request that he had ordered the charter. It is quite possible that Adelheid and Kunigunde knew each other for both were present at the diet of Aachen in 1000, Adelheid to become abbess of Santa Maria and Kunigunde to get married. There is another, closer connection. One of Kunigunde's most trouble-some brothers, Frederick of Luxemburg, was Adelheid's nephew by marriage, the husband of Gerberga, the daughter of Irmintrud and Adelheid's niece. It is not at all impossible that three so diverse women would gravitate towards each other: they were all about the same age, they were related by blood or marriage and their male relatives at various times produced great sorrow in their lives. The relationships between Kunigunde and Henry II and Gerberga and Frederick were not always peaceful. Although Adelheid was unmarried, she would have known of the troubles which her close friend, Archbishop Heribert of Cologne, had with the Emperor Henry II.

By the time of Adelheid's death in 1015, most of the original actors in the story of Vilich were all dead. It was time for a new generation. Here, too, the involvement of various well-connected women is of primary importance. The first was Adelheid's niece, her successor as Abbess of whom we know nothing, not even her name.[71] But we know a great deal more about another mid-eleventh century Vilich abbess, Mathilda, who built the third revision of the convent church. This energetic woman belonged to an amazing family on the fringes of the royal house which went by the name of the "Ezzonen."[72]

This important family originated with one Ezzo, or Erenfried,[73] who was born c. 955, the same year as Otto II. Ezzo's father was related to Ulrich, bishop of Augsburg, and the boy seems to have been educated there. Thietmar of Merseburg mentions Ezzo more or less in passing,[74] but the future Count Palatine is said to have been a close friend of the youthful Otto III: there is a story about a wild chess game at which Ezzo is said to have won the promise of a royal bride. The story might conceivably be relegated into the realm of fiction but for one very important reason: Ezzo did marry Mathilda, Otto II's youngest daughter. She had been educated at the abbey of Essen, then under the rule of the abbess Mathilda, a granddaughter of Otto I. The abbess was singularly reluctant to let her relative into the world, particularly to marry a tough and war-like frontier warrior such as Ezzo appears to have been from the account of him given in the story of the Brauweiler foundation. Indeed, Ezzo had to obtain Theophanu's royal command and produce a show of

force before he could collect his bride from Essen. The
marriage probably took place before 15 June 991, the death-
date of Theophanu.[75] Ezzo proved to be a faithful servant
both to Theophanu and to her son on a very volatile frontier.
He is usually referred to as Count Palatine of Aachen and his
family had some lands in the Lower Rhine area as well as in
Saxony and Thuringia.

Whatever misgivings Theophanu and the abbess of Essen
might have had concerning this marriage, and however great
was the disapproval of their contemporaries at this unequal
union, the union of Ezzo and Mathilda seems to have been a
love-match in spite of their age difference of twenty-three
years They produced ten children, three sons and seven
daughters. In 1024 Mathilda used her considerable dower
lands in the Rhine area to establish a monastery, Brauweiler
which served as the family church and mausoleum. She was
buried there upon her sudden death in 1025, aged forty-
seven. Ezzo survived his wife by nine years, dying in 1034
almost eighty years of age.

The children of Ezzo and Mathilda played an important
role in the history of the eleventh century. In 1002, upon the
death of their uncle Otto III, Ezzo put in a claim for the royal
crown on behalf of his wife and his sons. This effort came to
naught, as did a similar effort by Otto of Carinthia, a grandson of Otto I through his eldest daughter Liutgard.[76] The
crown went to the superior force, if not right, of Henry of
Bavaria, grandson of Otto I's brother Henry. Nevertheless,
this was fiercely resented in Aachen. It can probably be said
with some truth that Henry II sought to dislodge Ezzo, for the
Count Palatine had more than enough troubles with
Theodoric of Upper Lotharingia, another war-like frontier

noble and son of the dowager duchess Beatrice.[77] Henry II
had durable, if at times extremely volatile, relations with both
Lotharingia and Luxemburg, partially because he needed
some peace at the frontier with Capetian France and also
because Queen Kunigunde was a member of the family of
Luxemburg. Ezzo proved very adept at defending himself,
defeating Theodoric and imprisoning him. He also beat back
a challenge from Kunigunde's brothers and Henry II paid
Ezzo with the castle of Kaiserswerth to order to obtain the
release of Theodoric. The marriage in 1014 of Richeza, one of
Ezzo's daughters, to the Polish ruler Miesko II also had royal
approval. The matter of a possible claim to the throne was
resolved with a gift of land to Ezzo near Trier and a renunci-
ation of all claims to the royal crown by his family. This was
also beneficial to another claimant, Otto of Carinthia's grandson Conrad, who was a good friend of Ezzo's.[78]

Ezzo's ten children[79] would seem to have been a good
foundation for a new extended family with a solid power base
in the Lower Rhine area, but this did not happen. The eldest
son Liudolf who died in 1031 had two sons: Henry, who died
in 1033 without issue, and Conrad, duke of Bavaria, who died
in 1055 in disgrace and without heirs. The second son was
Hermann II, Archbishop of Cologne (1036–1056), a cleric
who had no family. The last son, Otto, died in 1047. Although he had no sons, he did have two daughters, Richeza,
who seems to have married into the Northeim family and
thus became one of the ancestors of the Welf family, and
Hildegard who died 1094/95 and who married Frederick of
Büren and thus became the great-grandmother of Frederick
Barbarossa. Of the seven daughters, only Richeza married,
and her son Casimir eventually became ruler of Poland.

When she was widowed in 1034, she returned to Germany, dying there in 1063. Her six sisters had entered the religious life and all became abbesses: Adelheid was at Nivelles and died before 1011; Sophie eventually at St. Maria in Mainz († 1027/31); Heylwig at Neuss († c. 1055); Theophanu at Essen (1039–1058); Mathilda at Vilich; and Diethofen († c. 1056); Ida at Santa Maria-im-Kapitol (†1060). Three of these abbesses—Theophanu, Ida, and Mathilda—are best known for their building projects: Theophanu built the famous western facade of the Minster in Essen; Ida was the major patron for the renovations at Santa Maria, and Mathilda was probably responsible for Vilich III.

There can be no doubt that the family of Ezzo and Mathilda was enormously powerful in the Rhine area, often in direct competition with the archdiocese of Cologne. When Hermann II became archbishop in 1036, the threat from Cologne was temporarily removed. The Ezzonen family power structure, however, did not survive beyond its creators. Though their buildings are beautiful and their cultural influence has lasted into our century, the "monastic daughters" of the House of Ezzo lacked the one element necessary to create a lasting dynasty: living heirs.

When Hermann II was succeeded by Anno II in 1056, the new Archbishop used every legal and illegal method to dislodge the Ezzo family from its position. He chose as his target the abbey of Brauweiler, the place where the remaining family wealth was centred and which was a very vulnerable target. When Richeza, the last Ezzo daughter, died in 1063, Anno II had her buried at the convent of St. Maria ad Gradus, his own foundation, and then used a stipulation in her will to deprive Brauweiler of her immense inheritance, particularly the rich manor of Clotten on the Mosel. In 1065, the newly elected abbot, Wolfhelm, brought suit against the archbishop, but Anno was an extremely powerful man and Brauweiler was not successful. The case continued beyond the death of Anno and to the end of Wolfhelm's life.[80] The somewhat cynical prologue of the *vita*, written by Bertha and edited by her brother, Wolfhelm, must in some way echo the frustration of the monks. Vilich, too, was vulnerable. Although not legally dependent upon Cologne, it was much too small to resist a determined take-over action. That this did not occur is probably due to its secular advocates, who themselves wished to use the benefits of Vilich's wealth, and thus prevented the Archbishop from interfering.[81]

The history of the Ezzo family illustrates a rather dangerous trend within aristocratic families of the Empire: their reluctance to allow their daughters to marry. Scholars are not at all certain what the reasons were: either the women themselves did not wish to marry, or their fathers and brothers did not wish to share the family wealth and power too widely. The lack, however, of male heirs and—to a lesser extent—of female ones destroyed the Saxon/Ottonian royal family and, as one scholar put it,[82] the noble houses probably did not fare any better. Men died in violent power struggles and their women, vowing chastity, retreated to the cloister to pray for the sins of their departed menfolk: not a recipe for the survival of a family.

There remain two other women who had connections to Vilich who belong mainly to the eleventh-century history of the abbey: one is Irmingard of Hammerstein, Adelheid's niece by marriage, and the other is of course Bertha, the author of the *vita*. There is no evidence at all to suggest that Irmingard

was ever at Vilich, although her marriage to Otto of Hammerstein probably took place before the death of Adelheid in
c. 1015. But her story, her family, and the problems that she
encountered in proving the legality of her marriage are inti-
mately connected to Vilich, not only in her own lifetime but
also because the historical evidence of her connection to her
husband's family comes partly from the *vita*.

Irmingard's life story can be pieced together from a variety
of sources and much is inferential, but the main outlines and
many of the details are well-known.[83] She was born probably
about 988—certainly not much later than 990—the daughter
of Godfrey the Prisoner, Count of Verdun, and his wife
Mathilda, daughter of Hermann Billung, duke of Saxony. The
dating of her birth is based on the fact that Godfrey was a
prisoner between 985 and 987. In the correspondence
between his wife and Gerbert of Aurillac there is no reference
to a daughter, although their five grown-up sons are mentioned.[84] Mathilda was in her forties when her daughter was
born and Godfrey was probably a decade older. Irmingard's
childhood and youth are also unknown. There is no record at
all of her until 1018 when, at the synod of Nymwegen, her
marriage to Otto of Hammerstein was challenged on grounds
of consanguinity. The couple countered the attack by assert-
ing that their union was not of recent date, so that it possibly
took place sometime after 1002, which is the earliest mention
we have of Otto, who was born c. 975. In 1018, neither partner of the marriage was exactly young, given the usual age for
marriage in their era: Otto was about forty-three and Irmingard thirty. It is presumed that their son Udo, who died in
1034, was not born until 1020: no children are mentioned at

the Nymwegen synod and at his death he was called *iuvenis,* a young bachelor.[85]

The complex story of the Hammersteiner divorce will be discussed in detail in Chapter V, but some final words on Irmingard should be said at this point. Her personality comes to life across the centuries through her efforts to save her marriage. The child of her parents' late middle age, she was an orphan by her early teens. Quite early in her life, she learned to rely solely on herself, for there is no record that her brothers, powerful nobles in Lotharingia, ever concerned themselves with her fate, at least not while she was married. It is thus quite possible that upon the death of her parents— about 1005 to 1008—she sought refuge with a well-known but quite distant relative, Abbess Adelheid, the daughter of her father's first cousin Gerberga. It is also possible that, since she did marry Otto of Hammerstein, she met him at Vilich, for there is no record that Otto ever went to Belgium, particularly since his grandfather Megengoz, whose lands were there, had died by 999. At that time Otto was a soldier in the imperial army and can be placed at the battle of "Mons Ungarius" against Arduin Marquis of Ivrea, which took place either in December of 1002 or early in 1003.[86] Whatever the time and place of their meeting, by 1018 the marriage of Otto and Irmingard had existed for some time. It was apparently a happy union since both partners vehemently protested the attempted dissolution. Irmingard proved again and again in the next five years that she had courage, skill, and persistence: she even traveled to Rome to appeal her case to the Pope.[87] Above all else she loved her husband, deeply and completely, and for his sake and for the sake of their union she was willing to defy archbishop, emperor and pope, even when the support she received from Otto was not always strong. Never passive in her actions, totally committed to her cause, her single-minded quest impressed her contemporaries and later historians alike. As a widow at the court of Henry III she was an honoured guest and one of the last records of her life is a mention of her in the *vita* of Poppo of St. Stablo, where she was asked to give some information about her native land, Lotharingia. A charter of Henry III of 1042 fixed the approximate time of her death.

The last character in this series of biographies is the author of the *vita*, the nun Bertha. Our knowledge of her family comes from the pen of Conrad, the author of the *Vita Wolfhelmi*, the biography of her brother, Abbot Wolfhelm of Brauweiler, who died in 1091. Their parents were Frumold, a noble, and his wife Eveza, called a daughter of Count Sicco. Wolfhelm was born early in the eleventh century and our first record of him is c. 1021 when he was a young monk at Trier. Since the comments about Bertha in Wolfhelm's *vita*[88] indicate that she was quite young when she wrote her famous work, her birth date might fall somewhere between 1020 and 1030, which would make her Wolfhelm's younger sister. Her reasons for coming to Vilich are unknown, but the choice of convent for the young noblewoman would seem appropriate since the Abbess Mathilda, probably at Vilich in the middle of the eleventh century, was a daughter of the founders of Brauweiler and possibly known to Bertha.

Whatever her reasons for coming to Vilich, Bertha was a member of the community from about 1050 to 1060 and here met and talked to the oldest sisters who had lived under the rule of Adelheid. In the *vita* Bertha mentions Engilrada:[89]from the testimony of this very elderly serving-maid come some of

the most vivid stories of Adelheid's life and make the life a
veritable gold-mine of scholarly information.

Bertha's death-date is not recorded but if she was born
about 1025, she could have survived as late as the end of the
eleventh century. She might be termed the last link in the
network of Vilich women. She was not related to the family
of Adelheid but her brother's connection with Brauweiler, the
family monastery of Ezzo and Mathilda and their children,
made it highly possible that she knew them. As Ezzo's
daughter, Mathilde, was probably abbess at Vilich when
Bertha was writing the *vita* of Adelheid there, the story has
returned to the royal family, to Theophanu and her daughters, to the Empress Adelheid and the Dowager Queen Mathilda and finally to Gerberga, the foundress of Vilich.

Vilich Abbey Church
1990

3 The Abbey: The Life of a Community; An Archæological Survey

B Y THE END OF THE TENTH CENTURY, THERE EXISTED IN THE kingdoms of Christian Europe numerous monastic communities of aristocratic women who had decided to remain single or as widows, had chosen to retire from the affairs of the world. Their reasons would have encompassed a wide range of possibilities: a genuine religious vocation, a desire to be free of the constraints put upon them by a society ruled mainly by men, a craving for learning, and perhaps fear of the pressures of family, marriage and childbirth. Within these well-organised, sometimes learned and frequently productive communities, women discovered in themselves a whole range of abilities which they were largely prohibited from exercising outside the cloister.[90]

Indeed, a cursory glance at the history of the early Christian Church shows that women were far more important to the workings of religious institutions than the male clerical establishment was willing to acknowledge. In early church rituals women were needed to fulfill tasks which could not be handled by men; this occurred mainly at the service of baptism but also in works of charity, mostly to aid other

women or children. These tasks were performed by "dedicated" virgins, widows of social standing or officially recognised helpers called deaconesses: as a group they were named
sanctimoniales. Such women are mentioned in the letters of
Paul, in the testimony of early church fathers; they are found
among the martyrs in the arena and in the pious legends of
the faithful.[91]

Women also participated in the earliest monastic communities. The aristocratic women to whom Jerome addressed
his letters on education and Christian morality lived such lives
of seclusion, contemplation, and service.[92] Religious communities for pious women were also established among the
newly christianised Germanic kingdoms of Europe. Inspired
by the Rule of St. Benedict and dressed plainly in habits of
black wool and simple white veils, they followed a path of
religious austerity and denial of the world's pleasures. Other
women, however, found that path too restrictive and created
their own rules of communal living and these women came
to be called "canonesses."[93]

In the eighth century, St. Boniface introduced the Christian religion to northern Germany, the centre of his mission-
ary work being the monastery of Fulda.[94] Charlemagne's
Saxon wars incorporated this area into his Christian state.
The main beneficiaries of this religious activity were aristocratic women who retired from the secular sphere in order to
live together in the *vita communis*. Their abbeys existed in
abundance in Saxony and Westfalia: Vreden, Freckenhorst
and Herford had eighth-century roots, Gandersheim and
Münster were started in the ninth century by members of the
Saxon aristocracy, and Quedlinburg owed its beginnings to
the activities of Mathilda Queen to Henry I.[95]

Lotharingia, Flanders, and the Rhine Valley had been christianised during the sixth and seventh centuries and a number
of female cloisters soon flourished in these Frankish heart-
lands. Though ecclesiastical life was disrupted in the early
ninth century by the political unrest which followed the
break-up of the Carolingian Empire and repeated Viking inva-
sions, the restoration of royal power in the tenth century
under the Saxon/Ottonian rulers of the new German realm
brought about an era of growth.

This rich female religious life was respected and revered
within the larger community, but it suffered some suspcion
about "irregularities" on the part of the leadership of the
church. In the reign of Louis the Pious, a group of such leaders led by Abbot Benedict of Aniane organised a thorough
monastic reform programme which led to the decrees of the
Council of Aachen in 816. The legislators took this opportunity to regularise female monastic communities, particularly the houses inhabited by canonesses which were not
ordered entirely according to the Benedictine rule [excised
bit]. There was strong opposition among noble familes to
these efforts to curtail or even eliminate the communities of
cannonesses and the end result was the creation of the
Institutio sanctimonialium, a rule akin in spirit to that of
Benedict, but presumed to have been created by Jerome in the
fourth century.[96]

Though the rules laid down at Aachen demanded that the
sisters eat together in the *refectorium* and sleep together in
dormitories, canonesses often had their own houses within
the monastic enclosure and only the young girls who were
attending the convent school prior to full membership in the
community actually lived together, usually under the super-

vision of the abbess. No formal vows were taken except possibly by the abbess, and the canonesses could return to the
world and legally marry. Other parts of the rule concerned
themselves with the activities of the sisters: their duty to
sing the services of the seven canonical hours every day,
their care of sick women and children and pilgrims, and
their communal life style generally.[97]

Vilich was a relatively late foundation of canonesses[98] and
its founders were not directly connected to the royal family. In
its charters, however, it had been granted the full immunities
of the royal abbeys of Quedlinburg, Gandersheim, and Essen,
the models for such religious establishments. Vilich's lands
and the appeal of the cult of Adelheid brought enough wealth
that the small community could carry out the wishes of the
founders throughout the centuries of its existence.[99]

Abbeys for canonessses were established by wealthy aristocratic families for, unlike male canons who made up the
majority of the cathedral priests and gained wealth from this
employment, canonesses had no priestly functions and rich
endowments of lands and incomes were needed for the abbeys
to survive. In Vilich the initial endowment came from the
patrimony of the deceased Godfrey, Adelheid's brother. From
references in the *vita*, it is evident that the remaining wealth
of her parents also came to Adelheid after their deaths and she
used this income for her charities. Some of the property of the
sisters would go to the abbey, although they could also retain
this wealth, using lay personnel to administer it for them.

The property of the abbey was administered by the abbess
and the chapter and feudal dues and services were paid to
them. A lay advocate represented the community in the lay
courts, an office either held by a local aristocrat or by the

family of the founder. Although necessary for the proper legal functioning of the convent, lay advocacy was expensive and later Vilich charters refer to several problems.[100]

The primary object of Vilich's existence was to provide a *vita communis* for the canonesses and the largest part of the wealth and the majority of the concerns of the abbess and her officials was directed to that end. Unfortunately there exists no description of the daily life in Vilich but from the *Institutio sanctimonialium,* from anecdotes in the *vita,* and from information gained from other such communities, a picture of the *vita communis* at Vilich in the early eleventh century does emerge.[101]

The Vilich community was not very large: there were about fifteen to twenty sisters at the onset and no more than thirty-five at its height. There was also a school for girls and a number of servants. In addition, a group of canons, priests who conducted the religious services for the canonesses as well as for visiting laity and pilgrims, lived in their own houses outside the abbey walls.[102]

Reception into such a community was not automatic and candidates were chosen carefully. In some instances the sisters themselves, or the abbess, made the selection. In the *vita,* Bertha addresses her second prologue to the resident canonesses and hopes that her efforts will please them enough to gain her full admittance to their circle.[103] Some candidates were proposed by the king, the local archbishop, or even the local aristocrat.[104]

In order to become a canoness, a young girl first entered the abbey school, usually at the age of seven. Such girls were called *puella* or *domicella.*[105] The duration of the schooling varied, but the earliest formal reception into the ranks of the

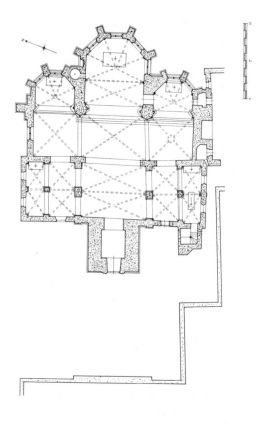

Vilich Abbey Church
Floor Plan c. 1000
[Artist's rendition]

Interior of the Abbey Church
c. 1000
[Artist's rendition]

canonesses was at age twelve to fourteen and often later. A ceremony marked this occasion, but canonesses did not take formal vows. Not every girl from the school became a canoness; some went only to receive an education and returned to their families, most probably to marry.[106]

The community of canonesses was led by the abbess or *abbatissa*. The rules of the Aachen council regard her as the sole authority over the congregation, its wealth, its buildings, its daily life, the conduct of its members and the discipline necessary for good order.[107] She was regarded as the *mater spiritualis*[108] of her charges and she was also a link between the community and the outside world, although she probably had a special chaplain to do those priestly functions which she was not allowed to perform.[109] The immunities granted by charter gave the Vilich community the right to elect their abbess, although there is a reference in one of the charters that she ought to be a member of the founders' family.[110] This was true in Adelheid's case and with her immediate successor, her niece, the case with the next abbess was, however, different. The connection of the family of Mathilda, daughter of Ezzo of Aachen, to the Vilich founders was quite remote and the family stipulation seems to have disappeared from use. However she was chosen, the abbess had to be free from too much outside interference in order that the community survive as a free institution. Although this was true of Vilich in the eleventh century, the abbey was too close to Cologne not to be influenced by its archbishop.

The new *electa* took an oath to follow the rules of the foundation; she usually also took a vow of chastity and received the benediction of the local bishop.[111] The stipulated age of a new abbess was to be forty but in the tenth and eleventh centuries this was rarely the case.[112]

The abbess was supported in her work by the chapter. In the eleventh century the terms *conventus* and *capitulum,* as well as *congregatio* or *collegium* were used for this regular assembly of the full members of the abbey which included all the canonesses as well as the canons (priests) of the abbey. The abbess presided at the meetings, although in her absence the provost *(praeposita)* or the dean *(decana)* could also take the chair. There was usually a chapter-house or *domo capitulari,* sometimes a hall situated above the refectory. Meetings were probably on a monthly basis and a bell was rung to gather the participants together. The discussions of the chapter concerned the important decisions pertaining to the life of the community: the election of a new abbess, the possible selection of an advocate, matters arising from churches under the abbey's control, matters pertaining to divine service, legal problems, matters pertaining to the property of the abbey, etc.[113] Decisions were sealed under the official seal of the community: in Vilich a seal exists from 1242 onward.[114] The canonesses could meet without the abbess and the canons regular met with their dean.

The abbess was assisted by five major officials and several minor ones. The major ones were called prelacies and consisted of the *praeposita,* the *decana,* the *custodissa* or *thesauraria,* the *scholastica,* and finally the *celleraria.* Minor offices were the *cameraria* and *portenaria* and their associates.

The *praeposita* or provost is mentioned in the Rules of Aachen as the substitute for the abbess when the abbess was absent from the convent. She was appointed by the abbess.[115]

The *decana* or dean was elected by the chapter. Her duties concerned the choir service of the community and all matters of minor discipline and the granting of six-week vacations to the canonesses. The dean also supervised the dormitories.[116]

The *custodissa/thesauraria* or custodian controlled the keys of the abbey. Her duties concerned the jewels, chalices, ornaments, bells and candelabras as well as the wine and the bread for communion and the holy water used in the church. A special duty of her office was the collection of tithes paid in beeswax for the making of candles. She also took care of the church/convent buildings and supervised the building of a new church or the renovation of an existing one.[117]

The *scholastica* or school mistress controlled the abbey school. The curriculum for the teaching of the *domicellae* was laid down in the rule of Aachen and encompassed moral teachings, the acquisition of fine manners, as well as the study of Latin, church history, the proper singing of the canonical hours and the liberal arts.[118] The abbess herself was often the *scholastica:* at Vilich Adelheid was concerned with the students and trained the canonesses for the choir.[119]

The *celleraria* or cellaress is mentioned in the *vita.* Her duties concerned the food and drink of the abbey and the supervision of the farms and vineyards which provided them. The *cameraria* or chamberlain was the main helpmate of the cellaress and did the accounts and supervised the kitchen and the kitchen servants.[120]

The *portenaria* or portress was usually an old and trustworthy canoness: she held the main keys of the abbey and locked the doors that led to the enclosures of the so-called immunity.[121] There were also many servants: the bath attendants, the washer women, gardeners, bakers, brewers. fishers etc. Some of these servants would have been men.[122]

The canonesses were to lead sober and industrious lives and were enjoined by the *Institutio sanctimonialium* to make their own clothes and take care of the sick and the poor.[123] But the primary duty of the canonesses was the *Dei ministerium,* the celebration of mass and particularly the seven canonical hours: matins/lauds *(matutina)*, prime *(prima)*, terce *(tertia)*, sext *(sexta)*, none *(nons)*, vespers *(vespertina)*, compline *(completoria)*. Numerous synods from the ninth century decreed that canonesses pray, read and listen and, above all, sing the offices of the church, particularly at night.[124] At Vilich, Adelheid herself led the choir and the story of the sister who could not keep a tune and who received a slap from the exasperated abbess is a very intimate view of life in this community.[125] In the beginning, the sisters at Vilich stood at the western end of the nave. In the early thirteenth century, a Gothic choir was built surrounding the older one, but the canonesses probably used a side altar, such as the chapel of Adelheid, for their private services. The main choir was used by the canons attached to the abbey who officiated at the Mass.[126]

The remaining time of the canonesses was spent in the *vita communis*, as symbolised by the use of a common dormitory,[127] and the use of a common refectory. The sisters were to keep silent at mealtimes and listen to readings from the Bible, but guests were welcomed. Canonesses also had their own "houses" within the convent and often they must have eaten privately, in small groups with guests, particularly after the renumeration for official positions was tied to food allowances and the common refectory was largely abandoned. There are references to food allowances in the *vita*, but not much in the way of specifics as to dining habits.[128]

Canonesses were allowed to travel, usually to visit their families. The normal time was six weeks but often they stayed away longer.[129] As canonesses were legally allowed to marry, such visits must have given families time to persuade a daughter or sister to remain in the world. The sisters wore secular clothing. Habits—usually a white linen tunic, a black wool cloak, and a loosely tied veil, white but with golden decorations—were worn mostly for church services even in the convent. It is not surprising that there were serving women such as Adelheid's maid Engelrada, for considerable time would have been spent on keeping such clothing clean.[130]

If great importance was attached to service in church and the communal life, so was the duty of helping the sick and the poor. Adelheid used her own wealth to establish charities. The Aachen rules demand that hospitals be part of the community service of the abbey: the pilgrims going to the altars of the saints came here as did the elderly. The supervisor of the hospital was a canon, a *magister hospitalis,* but one of the canonesses served as an almoner to aid him. A substantial part of the income of the abbey would go to pay for the charities.[131]

Another expenditure came from the construction of the church, the houses in which the sisters lived and other structures. The income of vacant "livings" was used for this purpose. Judging from the present house which was erected upon the mediæval foundations, Vilich was not very large. The buildings were probably surrounded by a wall both for protection and to establish the formal line of the legal immunity from the society surrounding it. Supervision for such building projects and the maintenance of the buildings was done by the custodian.[132]

Like other mediæval churches, Vilich's abbey church was not the work of a single period. Indeed, it was rebuilt and added to at least three times in its early history, renovated once again in the mediæval period, and rebuilt twice in the sixteenth and seventeenth centuries.

In 1944 the church was partially burned in the war, but the fire had not destroyed the outer walls. A thorough archæological examination of the building was undertaken in order to determine the various stages of construction. The information was used to establish the appearance of the original church buildings, the placement of the cloisters and the convent as well as confirm the documentary evidence from Vilich's past. Undertaken by the University of Bonn and the Rheinisches Landesmuseum and under the directorship of Irmingard Achter,[133] the survey began in 1949 and continued until 1955.

The church of St. Peter at Vilich is located at the highest point of a large plain consisting of a triangle formed by the confluence of the Rhine and the Sieg and is on the eastern side of the Rhine, directly across the river from Bonn. The village and manor of Vilich were older than the abbey. The archæological survey dug up the remains of a Frankish cemetery (fifth to eighth century) and the earliest Vilich church was placed in the midst of this cemetery. Remains of this small church were found within the fabric of the present church, for all later church buildings followed the original placement of nave and altar. This early church was erected in the eighth or ninth century and was used by the founders of the abbey when they began their construction c. 980. The original building was a rectangle about 6 m long and 5,30 m wide. Sometime later—probably in the tenth century—another room was added, about 3,80 m wide and 4,70 m in depth. The addition was used as a chancel. This small church, the basis of all future buildings, had served the Vilich manor and was probably the proprietory church, the *Eigenkirche,* of that estate. This church and manor belonged to Megengoz and Gerberga in 980, and formed a part of the original property from which the abbey took its wealth. The inclusion of this small church within the much larger Abbey was based upon the desire to retain the consecrated altar, dedicated to

Saints Cornelius and Cyprian. This *patrocinium* is also attested for the first abbey church.[134]

Vilich II, the first abbey church, was finished by 987, the time of the first imperial charter. The driving force behind the foundation of the abbey and the building of the church was Gerberga, Adelheid's mother. The church had a single nave, about 9 m wide and 25,10 m long. In the form of a *Westwerk*, the main entrance was at the western side. The choir was at the eastern end and contained the chancel of the original church. A cloister, added somewhat later, was located at the south side of the church. There is evidence of a small annex to the choir which eventually became part of the crypt. This annex was probably the site of the burials of Gerberga, †c. 996, and Megengoz, †c. 999. A lost inscription located the tomb of the founders within the walls of the church; the burial may also have included the remains of their son Godfrey and their daughters Irmintrud and Bertrada.[136]

The early manor or cemetery church (Vilich I) and the first abbey church (Vilich II) with the simple rectangular hall and the added rectangular sanctuary and/or choir was constructed in the basic form used by Christian churches everywhere in northwestern Europe. Although the dimensions might change (some do not even have the added choir), this model was used from the earliest times of Christian worship in this area—i.e. from the fifth century—and continued to be used, mainly by rural parish churches, until the thirteenth century.[136] The oldest Vilich building stood in a cemetery centuries older. This too was typical since Christian cemeteries appeared on Frankish manors as the earliest manifestations of Christian worship, closely followed by the building of a cemetery church, usually a proprietory church owned by the lord of the manor. The connection between Christian worship and the dead led to the tradition of the burial of important members of the community within the church. Vilich, the burial place of Adelheid, became a cult centre almost as soon as the abbess had died.[137]

The second building, superimposed upon the first, was Vilich II, the original abbey church, constructed c. 980. It had a single nave with a rectangular choir. This was a common form in this area and was used both in large and small buildings. Vilich II may, however, have been the last use of the old rectangular hall, since the church of St. Pantaleon in Cologne, reconstructed about the same time, was built as a basilica, an architectural form imported from Italy and the building form of the near future.

Written evidence from Vilich speaks directly only about the tenth-century building. Since the archæological survey of the Vilich church showed a massive reconstruction in the eleventh century, the affirmation of such actions can only be made by inference. The survey established that the second abbey church, Vilich III, was constructed on the site of the first and that the old wall foundations were used for the pillars of the central nave. The *Westwerk* remained but the entrance may have been moved to the north side.[138]

What did Vilich III look like?[139] The central nave was still 9 m wide, each of the side naves were 3,65 m wide and this is still true today though two chapels were added later. The ceiling was flat and the height has been estimated at about 10,80 m, which is suitable for the 9 m width. Since the seventeenth-century rebuilding, the new height is 12,65 m, not impossible for Vilich III as well. The rectangular transcepts and the semi-circular sanctuary/chancel were added at this point; below it was a *Ringkrypta*[140] so that the altar now rose about 1,80 m above the floor of the nave and had eleven or twelve steps.

This crypt was disturbed by the erection of the Gothic choir in the thirteenth century, but its remains offer clues as to why the second abbey church was built so soon after the original one. The cult of Adelheid attracted so many pilgrims that the old church was no longer adequate. In the *vita*, Bertha describes the transfer of Adelheid's remains to a tomb within the church from its original site in the cloister.[141] The sandstone sarcophagus, which forms her tomb today, was confirmed by the archæological survey as the original one. This had been located under the floor from which it was moved in the early thirteenth century to the Adelheid-chapel. The south transcept, possibly on the site of the original cloister where Adelheid was first buried, was always especially marked.

When exactly was Vilich III, the second abbey church, built? The answer to this question depends on indirect evidence from the written records, as well as proof from the archæological survey. The first evidence comes from the papal bull of 24 May 996 where there is a reference to a *"monasterium ancillarum dei in honore sanctorum martirum cornelii et ciprieni,"*[142] an affirmation that the saints Cornelius and Cyprian were indeed the patrons of the original abbey church, both Vilich II as well as Vilich I, the old Frankish manor church. The second indicator is the death date of Adelheid, usually given as 1015, a tradition which is very old although the year of her death is not recorded in the *vita*. There is, however, evidence that she was still alive in 1003 and also that she was dead in 1021. The *vita* records her death as taking place in Cologne at St. Maria-im-Kapitol and describes her burial at Vilich.[143]

After Adelheid's death, miracles began to happen at her tomb which were witnessed and recorded by Bertha in the *vita* and she adds that the many pilgrims so disturbed the sisters in the cloister that it became necessary to rebury Adelheid's remains in the abbey church. As pilgrims continued to come, the abbey church soon became too small to hold them. Bertha describes the decision to build a new church as well as the fact that the second abbey church was to be dedicated to St. Peter.[144] The archæological survey shows that this new church was built around the old one, gradually incorporating parts of it into the new building. The measurements of the central nave remained the same. The new church resembled a pillared basilica very common in this region in the first part of the eleventh century. The *Ringkrypta,* now also containing the tomb of Adelheid, remained to allow the pilgrims to venerate the saint.[145]

Why the new church was dedicated to a new patron is not entirely clear. Vilich, although granted immunities and freedoms from episcopal control in its charters, was nevertheless much influenced by Cologne. Archbishop Heribert (†16 March 1021) had held Adelheid in high esteem and her position as abbess of Santa Maria, where she succeeded her sister Bertrada, brought her into close contact with the affairs of the archbishopric. According to much later testimony,[146] the abbess of Santa Maria sat in the chapter of the cathedral as the first among the abbesses; whether this was already true in the eleventh century is not known. The *vita* records that Heribert put Adelheid in charge of poor relief in times of famine. Thus the new dedication may have originated in Cologne as the old cathedral there was also dedicated to this saint and it could be interpreted as a sign of a renewed loyalty to Rome.[147] The construction of Vilich III took place as early as the 1020's and as late as the 1040's. The principal "builder" was undoubtedly the abbess Mathilda, although Bertha does not name her in the *vita.*[148]

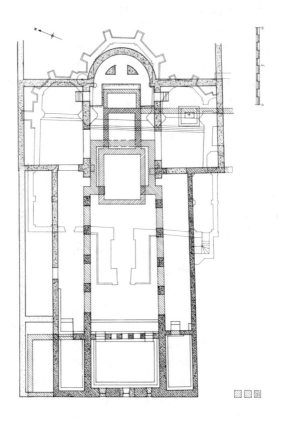

Vilich Abbey Church
Floor Plan 1990
[Artist's rendition]

Vilich Abbey Church
1990

The twelfth and thirteenth centuries brought further changes to this church, such as the vaulted ceiling as well as the addition of a Gothic choir which destroyed the old *Ringkrypta* at the eastern end. The sarcophagus of the saint was moved into a chapel built especially for that purpose: the *Adelheidis-Kapelle* is one of the most beautiful parts of the extant church. There was enough renovation done to label this building Vilich IV. The enormous expense of this project put Vilich's finances in a precarious state. The convent was "rescued' by the Archbishop, but the price of this help was control of its affairs by Cologne.[149]

In 1583, and again in 1632, the abbey's very existence was threatened. But the church survived. The choir and the transcepts were rebuilt in 1596/97 but the nave was not finished until 1605. The 1632 destruction necessitated more extensive changes: the nave was shortened considerably and a tower was added at the west entrance. The outer shape of this reconstruction, completed between 1699 and 1701, has remained to the present day. When the Bollandists came to open the sarcophagus of the Saint in the middle of the seventeenth century, the tomb was found to be empty: no one knows what happened to the remains. Nevertheless the chapel and the tomb were renovated in 1762.

The ancient abbey ceased to exist as a community on 4 September, 1802 and its lands and possessions, including some elegant silver altar ware, went to the princely house of Nassau-Usingen. The sisters were given until 24 April, 1804 to find other accommodations and after their departure, the abbey church became the parish church of St. Peter of Vilich. In 1871 a new altar to Adelheid was consecrated and in 1872 the sarcophagus was raised above ground and a seventeenth-century recumbant figure of the saint was placed upon it. This figure is in that place still. It shows Adelheid dressed in the robes of a "princess of the empire with crown" in seventeenth-century style, holding a staff of office.[150]

The present interior of the church at Vilich is a careful reconstruction done between 1955 and 1965. The transcepts and the choir are mediæval and the nave is the size of the seventeenth-century building. The outside of the church had always been plastered, as was indicated from traces found on the stones. The mediæval part is painted a reddish tint which was the surviving colour; the nave and the steeple are painted white in the style of the seventeenth century

Canonesses and their communities endured as a vital part of the German monastic tradition in spite of official disfavour.[151] Though few of the cloisters survived the Reformation and the remaining ones were secularised in the early nineteenth century, their churches, often lovingly restored, still exist in our time. They have become the parish churches of the towns and villages that had grown up around the original mediæval abbeys.

Detail from the sarcophagus of Adelheid of Vilich
in the choir of the Vilich Abbey Church

4 *Vita Sanctæ:* The Life & Times of St. Adelheid of Vilich

*Let us begin the work with an exhortation of the Holy Spirit
who has affected all good things which have existed. So this
work also should be finished through the support of his gifts,
for therein lies the beginning and the end of all good. If we
consider our insignificance and inexperience, then we tremble
at the attempt to begin a great work. But if we look to the
bounty of divine reward, then the fear disappears, for the
Spirit blows where he wills as the gospel testifies. We have
faith that he will fill this writing with his breath, because of
the merits of our Mother, the holy Lady Adelheid. The praise-
worthy chain of her life we, her lowliest maids, are trying to
describe here, and we pray, that the Holy Spirit may enflame
the spark of intelligence which nature has given us.*[152]

AFTER THE PROLOGUES—BOTH THE TONGUE-IN-CHEEK ONE TO
Anno of Cologne[153] and the genuine one to the sisters
of the abbey of Vilich—this is how Bertha begins her
biography of Adelheid. In the style of her time, she invokes
the Holy Spirit; alive to the conventions of her age she begs
humble pardon for her audacity that she, young and inex-
perienced, should undertake so momentous a task as the

writing of this biography. But beyond all these stylised words, there is a clear and inquiring mind at work. Trained in Latin and capable of producing an elegant rhymed prose in that language, Bertha sets about her endeavour with candour and ability. She has a mission: to tell the story of the holy virgin Adelheid, a woman she had never met but whose presence she encountered through the testimony of older inmates of Vilich and through the miracles she herself witnessed. Bertha's book was written about 1057, some forty years after Adelheid's death, but she managed to put together in her short work the living memory of the community at Vilich.[154]

Biographies written in the Middle Ages are not always as historically useful as the might seem at first reading; they abound in quotations from classical sources which were thought appropriate but which obscure the historical reality of the events described.[155] The problem is compounded when these biographies concern the lives of saintly men and women. A *vita* is not usually written to detail an historical incident or to portray an historical personage. Rather, its purpose is to describe a faith journey. It is for this reason that these lives are often patterned on preconceived notions of what a holy life should be. Incidents may be invented or enlarged, stories retold many centuries after the event, and authors know little about the era or the events they are describing. The resulting biographies are moving exemplars of extraordinary faith as well as important literary sources, but they pose difficulties for historians who seek details of events which are secular rather than sacred.[156]

Some of the biographies written in the tenth and eleventh centuries, however, come out of a tradition of historical literature produced within living memory. Indeed, their writers were very conscious of their historical mission. Though allowing for some exaggeration and without denying their deep religious stance or literary value, these lives are historically viable portraits.[157] The Vita Adelheidis falls into this category. In detailing the family history of the Vilich foudners and in relying upon the testimony of eye-witnesses, Bertha has produced a valuable historical source and has created a vivid portrai of its central character.[158]

Adelheid was the youngest daughter of Megengoz and Gerberga, founders of Vilich.[159] Her birth date is usually given as 970 and the description of her youthfulness at her installation as abbess bears this out.[160] Whether she was seventeen or somewhat older in 987 cannot be established with certainty, but she was evidently much younger than her brother and sisters and her parents were middle aged at the time of her birth.[161]

Adelheid entered the Convent of St. Ursula in Cologne at an early age and Bertha discusses her education there as a child.[162] She was probably there in 977 when her only brother was killed and when her parents began to build the church at Vilich to commemorate his death. They used their manor as the basis for their new foundation[163] and, when completed, Gerberga assembled suitable candidates for her new cloister. It was then that she "redeemed" her daughter Adelheid from St. Ursula with a gift of land, so that the young woman could become abbess at Vilich. Gerberga's first plan was to make the new house a Benedictine nunnery, but Adelheid resisted this, exclaiming that she preferred the white linen habit of the canonesses to the black wool of the nuns. Gerberga accepted her daughter's wish. Bertha commenta that God took no offence as he deemed a willing sacrifice more important than a forced one.[164]

In 987 Megengoz and Gerberga appealed to the royal government to give a charter to Vilich and thus establish a legal identity for the new convent. Bertha writes that the charter of immunities was issued by Otto III and that it

granted Vilich all the privileges, protections, and legal freedoms that were associated with the imperial convents of
Gandersheim, Quedlinburg, and Essen. No judges or advocates
could intrude upon the convent without the permission of
the abbess and the congregation and the abbess was to be
freely elected by the chapter. This charter as well as a papal
bull issued in 996 and an reaffirmation by Henry II in 1003
must have been in the cloister archives for Bertha says that
they are "faithfully preserved in our custody."[165]

These charters and others pertaining to the abbey are
found today in a box marked Vilich and stored in a basement
corner of the *Staatsarchiv* in Düsseldorf. The 987 charter is
written in a fine but legible hand. It tells the story of great
court held at Andernach in January 987, a diet of princes and
bishops presided over by the seven-year-old Otto III and his
mother, the Dowager-Regent Theophanu. Others present
were the Dowager-Empress Adelheid, Archbishop Heribert of
Cologne and Bishop Notker of Liège. Gerbert of Aurillac had
expected to attend, but problems kept him at Rheims.
Megengoz and Gerberga came to this meeting with their petition, probably accompanied by their daughter Imiza whose
friendship with Theophanu has already been noted. Imiza's
husband was Heribert, Lord of Hammerstein, and their castle
is but a short distance from Andernach. The Vilich charter is
dated 18 January.[166]

The papal bull was issued by Gregory V on 24 May 996, but
the document in the Vilich collection is a copy, possibly
made in the early eleventh century at Vilich. It confirms the
987 provisions with some adjustments and records that the
death of Gerberga was a recent occurrence.[167]

The 1003 charter of Henry II only exists in a transsumpt
copy made for King Adolf of Nassau on 7 July 1292.[168] Queen
Kunigunde, the wife of Henry II, is named as intercessor and

Adelheid is named as abbess. This charter is the last documentary evidence of Adelheid in her own life time.

The first phase of the growth of Vilich came to an end with
the death of Gerberga about 995. Adelheid, now in her late
twenties, was faced the enormous task of following in her
mother's footsteps and acting on her own without the advice
and counsel of an experienced administrator. Nor did she
have the support of her father who continued to live in
Geldern. Bertha's description of Adelheid's actions at that
moment recall vividly the loneliness the young woman must
have felt. It is precisely at that point that Adelheid decided—
perhaps in memory of her mother, perhaps also to do
penance for a perceived sin and to please God with her
humility—to change the rule of the abbey from the observances of the canonesses to the more stringent rule of St.
Benedict.[169] But in this she was not immediately successful
and her chapter refused to agree and she even lost some of her
canonesses. Supported by her sister, Abbess Bertrada of Santa
Maria in Cologne, Adelheid was undaunted by the opposition
and continued in her quest to turn Vilich into a Benedictine
nunnery.[170] It is hardly surprising that Bertha felt sympathy
with Adelheid's Benedictine vision since she had been influenced by the stricter reform tradition that had swept through
the Rhineland in the early eleventh century. This mood is
reflected in her analysis of Adelheid's actions.[171]

Two further incidents were to affect the life of Adelheid
profoundly in the five years after her mother's death. The first
was the death of her father;[172] the second was her election as
abbess of Santa Maria.[173]

According to the *vita*, Megengoz outlived his wife by three
years. He died about 999 at his home in Geldern and Adelheid
had his remains buried at Vilich, Bertha recalls the story of his
daughter's vision of him on the night he died, 24 May accord-

ing to tradition. Bertha records a further vision: he appeared to one of the sisters saying that he was now at peace and in eternal joy. The remains of a small crypt which might have been the tomb of Gerberga and Megengoz were found in the 1955 excavations and there is some evidence that the relics were still within the convent as late as the sixteenth century. A violent local war in the 1580's severely damaged the church and probably also destroyed any relics or burial remains. Adelheid's body may also have been taken from her sarcophagus at that time.[174]

At Megengoz' death Adelheid inherited a large share of the family wealth. Her sister Imiza had died earlier and there is no evidence of any claim by the Hammerstein siblings or by Adelheid's remaining sister. Adelheid made careful provisions for the use of her inheritance. Some of the lands went for the use of the convent, but Bertha also describes the plans that Adelheid made for charitable donations to the poor. Fifteen beggars were to be fed and clothed from the profits of one manor in perpetuity; fifteen solidi of money were to be given to them at Christmas. Another fifteen beggars were to be looked after by the convent and these were to receive a sum of money at Lent, as well as payments on the feastdays of the Apostles and at three of the quarter-days. It is interesting that Adelheid's own feast day, 5 February, falls just before Lent. These charitable bequests were still in force in 1804 when the sisters were expelled from the abbey by Duke Frederick Augustus of Nassau-Usingen. Bertha notes that she had written down these provisions carefully so that the matter "would not fall into oblivion."[175]

The death of Adelheid's sister Bertrada about 1000 further changed her life. Archbishop Heribert of Cologne, who knew the sisters, apparently wanted Vilich's abbess to undertake the governance of Santa Maria. Adelheid, who must have appreciated the enormous work load, was not too eager to

comply. Bertha stresses that this was further evidence of the
genuine humility of the abbess but the burden of frequent
trips across the Rhine river—possibly in an open boat—to
administer the much larger Santa Maria could easily have
been a deciding factor. Heribert, however, had his way. He
took his proposal to the emperor who happened to be at
Aachen and forthwith Adelheid was called to the court and
confirmed in her new office. Straightforward as this tale
seems to be, it is not without its problems. Bertha does not
give the name of the emperor nor the date of Bertrada's
death.[176] Scholars have suggested various dates around the
year 1000. Sometimes it is set in the reign of Henry II, possibly in view of the confirmation of the Vilich charter in 1003
which would date Adelheid's abbacy from 1002 when
Henry II was in Aachen, but not yet an emperor, or from
1014, when Henry II was again in Aachen. Henry, however,
had little reason to give additional power to an obscure lady
from a small convent, especially when he knew that she
belonged to a family which he disliked intensely. Nor was
Henry particularly fond of Heribert of Cologne who had been
merely lukewarm to Henry's assumption of the German
crown in 1002.[177] If 1015 was indeed Adelheid's death date,
the 1014 date for her abbacy at Santa Maria does not fit, for
according to the *vita* the duration of her tenure in Cologne
was considerably longer than a few months.

All these problems disappear if the events are set in the
Aachen court of Easter 1000 which Otto III was holding
before he left on his fateful final trip to Italy. Furthermore,
Heribert had the assurance that his imperial friend would
grant any reasonable request, for the archbishop had been
chancellor of Italy and stood high in Otto's favour. Adelheid
was certainly known to the young ruler and he had met other
members of her family. Details of the meeting between the
almost twenty-year-old ruler, tall as his Saxon ancestors but

with dark eyes and hair and the quick temper of his mother's Greek heritage, and the thirty-plus abbess in her white robes, with a shyness of manner as one unused to grand occasions such as royal courts, have not been preserved for posterity. It is entirely possible that Adelheid did meet the future King Henry II at Aachen at the same time, for the then duke of Bavaria was in Aachen on the occasion of his marriage to Kunigunde of Luxemburg. The latter was also a sort of kinswoman to the abbess: Frederick of Luxemburg, one of Kunigunde's brothers, was married to Adelheid's niece, a sister of Otto of Hammerstein.[178]

Adelheid returned to Vilich both more powerful and more burdened. Indeed, says Bertha, the work she used to do in secret and without much fanfare at Vilich now became very public at Cologne. Heribert sought her advice and Bertha calls their relationship one of *caritas.* In the first decade of the eleventh century there were several bad harvests in the Cologne area[179] and Bertha describes Adelheid's actions during one of these times of need.

> Touched by their great need, Adelheid herself cared with devotion for everyone. To the healthy and robust she parcelled out bread and bacon; to the ill she served cabbage and vegetables carefully boiled with meat. The dying and those despairing of life she revived with broths mixed with water and flour and other nourishment, always watching with diligence that the body would not be put into peril by overeating after the lack of proper food.[180]

The abbess of Santa Maria was indeed the leading nun in Cologne. The *vita* calls her "that saintly woman, so remarkable, so great and religious, leading the choir of virgins" and Heribert "that eager imitator of St. Peter." Bertha summarises her comments about Adelheid's work in this way:

> For this venerable abbess, lady and mother of virgins, whom the heavenly Father had put in charge of the many, after she had been faithful over the few, watched carefully and diligently over her double herd, following the example of the good Shepherd. At all times she repeated in her secret heart the words of the Gospel, "Everyone to whom much is given, of him will much be required."

The responsibilities which kept Adelheid in Cologne far outstripped those in Vilich, and her "hands-on" kind of government—the true essence of her personality—must have increased her labours to a great extent. To add to her troubles, the sisters at Vilich were often very jealous of the time their abbess spent in Cologne, although Adelheid took care to divide her time equally between the two locations.[183]

These heavy responsibilities and the frequent travel finally took their toll. Bertha only records the date of Adelheid's death, 5 February, not the year of her death. She must have heard the details from the sisters at Vilich who recalled them frequently, all the more so because their beloved lady and mother had died so far away from them, in Cologne.[184]

The beginning of February was not the best time to cross a river as wide and fierce as the Rhine nor to go travelling, as Adelheid did, in a cart or even on horse back. On the evening of the feast day of St. Blaise, right after a meal, she was struck down with a severe sore throat and after Compline she mentioned her ailment to Ida, a sister from Vilich and her travelling companion. Ida, however, did not take the matter seriously and returned to her "warm bed." Adelheid, however, seems to have had a premonition of death and after a sleepless night, she went to the church and after Communion requested that Archbishop Heribert should come to her. The archbishop had been her friend and advisor and the sight of Adelheid so weak and ill affected him greatly. Messengers were sent to Vilich telling the sisters that their abbess was ill and that they should come quickly to see her. But apparently the Vilich sisters, like young Ida, were not totally convinced of the seriousness of the illness and delayed their departure for Cologne,. It was in this way that they arrived too late to see their beloved mother alive.

Heribert had probably planned to have Adelheid interred in Cologne, but the sisters fell on their knees before him and begged him to release her earthly remains for burial in Vilich. This he eventually granted, and the sisters took the body across the river on the feastday of St. Agatha and buried it in the Vilich cloisters, as Adelheid herself had requested.

Details of death and burial are prominent in the biographies of saints; particularly of those who died a martyr's death. In Adelheid's case the description has more in common with the death-scenes of other important people of her era and there is little of the miraculous and the extraordinary, except for one bit of memory that the convent inhabitants must have cherished through the years. When the sisters placed the body of their abbess on the boat that was to take them across the Rhine, they realised that they would have to row a considerable distance upstream, no mean feat in the middle of winter. But as soon as they were ready to start, the vessel took off on its own accord. This was the first miracle Bertha recorded after the death of Adelheid.[185]

The last six chapters of the *vita* consist of *miracula*, a description of miracles which happened at Adelheid's grave: first at her burial place in the cloister and later at her tomb, when her remains were interred in the crypt under the altar of the convent church. Although Bertha took some of her stories from the memories of older sisters, she herself experienced some of them. These miracles cast some light on the great compassion Adelheid had for the suffering during her life-time. Two of these stories are particularly poignant.

The first[186] concerns an unnamed nobleman who had committed a very serious crime for which he was put into chains by papal decree and told to seek forgiveness at various shrines until such time as a holy person would take pity on him and release his bonds. He arrived at Vilich during the abbacy of Adelheid's successor, her niece. It was during his sojourn at Vilich that his bonds were shattered and those of his brother who had helped him to carry this great burden. Bertha then describes, as she often does, the very real after-math of this miracle. For the saint had loosened the chains, but it took careful nursing to restore nearly dead arms and legs to their former strength. When the two brothers were able to leave, the abbess gave them new clothes to wear and horses to ride and sent them to their homeland. In some ways this is an extraordinary story and it is regrettable that Bertha did not mention the brothers' names nor the country of their origin. Perhaps she did not know it because it did not seem to be important to the convent. What strikes us today about this story is not the release of the nobleman's bonds, but the action of his brother who selflessly and from great love helped his sinful brother to carry his chains.

The other miracle concerns[187] a child who suffered from a crippling disease of spasms called "Little's disease,"[188] perhaps the result of brain damage due to premature birth or inade-quate care of a premature infant. After the child, a nine-year old boy, was cured through a vision of Adelheid, he requested his parents to take him to Vilich so that he could say his prayers at her tomb. During the journey, the horse upon which the boy was riding lost its footing and jumped into the river, probably the Sieg which flows near Vilich. The parents, following on foot, were disconsolate since they feared that their son had drowned so soon after having been restored to health. After an hour, however, the horse and the child reappeared and, rejoicing and giving great praise for God's mercy, they continued to the convent. Bertha's description of the child's affliction is accurate enough for a modern doctor to recognise the symptoms of Little's disease. In this instance, as in so may others, she proves to be an acute observer of details and practical fine points.

Bertha's attention to detail can also be noted in her descriptions of the personality of her central character. Jacob Schlafke, the German translator of the *vita*, called Adelheid *"eine rheinische Frohnatur,"* impulsive, open to all good influences, rarely concerned with self and always concerned for others.[189]

Adelheid was a truly involved leader. Since her convent, true to the calling of canonesses, was much concerned with education, she visited the convent school frequently and taught and examined the young scholars.[190] She was also interested in the liturgical life of the convent and worked with the sisters on the proper methods of singing the offices. One of these sisters could not carry a tune. It is not given to everyone, comments Bertha, to be able to do everything. The abbess eventually lost her patience with the errant singer and boxed her ears, an impulsive action that she must have immediately regretted but one which endowed the so corrected sister with true pitch.[191]

At other times Adelheid could be observed caring for the young girls in the school dormitories, secretly bringing them a snack after hours. She was always concerned with the sick, even those who pretended illness, and often admonished them that their time in bed would be better spent if they used their hands to advantage. Coming back from one of her trips to Cologne, she would call all the Vilich sisters to see her and ask them questions about what had happened in her absence.[192]

Finally there is the story of the cellaress whose presence was requested by the abbess just as she was in the process of opening a barrel of wine. She obeyed without hesitation and arrived with the stop of the casket in her hand, having forgotten to close off the flow of the wine. Adelheid comforted her distressed official and together the two women went into the cellar to survey the damage. To their amazement, no wine had spilt from the casket. The cellaress praised the great sanctity of her abbess to which she ascribed this miracle, but Adelheid answered that the miracle had occurred because the cellaress had obeyed her superior's command without hesitation, as a true nun should. Modern scepticism aside, this story adds one more detail to the personality of the abbess and reveals her conscientious and kind nature.

Though less powerful than Theophanu of Essen or Mathilda of Quedlinburg and less well-known than Hrotsvit of Gandersheim or Hildegard of Bingen, Adelheid of Vilich nevertheless holds a place of honour in their midst. Capable, practical, loved by those in her charge and revered and respected by those in authority, Adelheid was a person of outstanding presence. Doubtless it was this presence that attracted Bertha to write her biography and what kept her memory alive in her convent throughout the centuries.

In 1966 the cult of St. Adelheid of Vilich was confirmed by Pope Paul VI after a process of canonisation that had begun in 1917. Her feast day remains 5 February, the day of her burial.[194]

Seal of Vilich Abbey Church

5 A *Cause Célèbre:* Otto & Irmingard of Hammerstein & the Laws of Marriage: A Postscript to the *Vita*

B ERTHA'S MID-ELEVENTH CENTURY *VITA ADELHEIDIS* RECORDS the living memory of the saintly abbess of Vilich and sets down the miracles that supported her cult. When the *vita* was included in the thirteenth-century legendaries in which the earliest surviving manuscripts of the text survive, Adelheid was venerated as a local saint in the lower Rhine area. Perhaps the compiler of these legendaries found the manuscript in the library of the monastery of Brauweiler, a discovery which accounts for its inclusion in the collection.[195] When the editors of the *Monumenta Germaniæ historica* included the *Vita Adelheidis* in the fifteenth volume of the *Scriptores,* their purpose was a scholarly one. Bertha had written a splendid Latin life and it fitted neatly with the other biographies of the tenth and eleventh centuries.

This could easily have been the end of the interest in the *vita.* Bertha, however, had included a rather intriguing family history in the opening chapters of her life of Adelheid, a history which, as the various authors of the *Jahrbücher des deutschen Reiches* were possibly the first to notice, seemed to give at least a partial answer to one of the more interesting historical puzzles from the early eleventh century: the story of the Hammersteiner divorce. For almost a century, scholars showed little interest in Adelheid and Vilich[196] but the story of Otto and Irmingard of Hammerstein had become an important topic in the scholarship relating to the reign of Henry II.[197]

What explains this attraction? Is it perhaps the intimate glimpse into the personal lives of two people? Or is there another reason? In his *Geschichte der sächsischen Kaiserzeit*, Robert Holtzmann, a sober historian rarely given to hyperbole, analysed the marital fortunes of the Hammersteiner couple and wrote glowingly about the eternal power of love which triumphed over empire and church.[198] In the Annales Quedlinburgenses, the anonymous author, certainly a partisan of the Emperor Henry II, raved about Otto's "insane lust" that drove the count to attempt to kidnap an archbishop.[199] For all that he was a devoted cleric, Thietmar of Merseburg, a relative of the Hammersteiner and the leading historian in Germany about 1000, spoke feelingly about human love.[200] The tenacity with which Otto of Hammerstein and Irmingard of Verdun clung to each other shocked and exasperated their contemporaries, for expressions of human love were rarely so public in that era. It is possibly that tenacity which has also caught the interest of modern historians.

The main incidents of the Hammersteiner divorce took place at least three years after Adelheid's death, but it is entirely possible that the abbess knew both of them. Otto was the youngest son of her elder sister Irmintrud and not much younger than Adelheid herself. Irmingard was the daughter of Adelheid's grandmother's first cousin and thus counted as a kinswoman.[201]

On 16 March 1018, the Emperor Henry II (1002–1024) held a synod and diet at the imperial city of Nymwegen, now in the Netherlands. To this court he summoned Otto of Hammerstein, Count of the Wetterau, and his wife Irmingard, daughter of Godfrey the Prisoner, the late Count of Verdun.[202] The purpose of this summons was the emperor's accusation that the couple were living together in an illegal union and that they were too closely related for their marriage to be licit. The sources go into few details: they indicate that this was not the first time the emperor had made this accusation, that the emperor demanded an end to the proceedings and that the synod dutifully annulled the marriage on grounds of consanguinity.[203]

Annulments of marriages on this ground are not infrequent and they usually arise from the desire of one partner—often the husband—to rid himself of the other partner—often the wife. But in this instance, such was not the case. The annulment was put into action by the emperor and supported by the archbishop of Mainz, Erkenbald, in whose diocese Otto's county was located.

The case was further complicated by the fact that the couple refused to comply with the action of the synod. They protested that their marriage was not a recent one and they saw no reason why they should not be married. Indeed, Otto attempted to sway the authorities by a personal appeal at a diet in Bürgel in June of that year when "he begged the emperor on bended knee" to rescind the verdict. To no avail. Both Henry II and the archbishop remained adamant and threatened the petitioner with excommunication, outlawry, and the loss of all his possessions.[204]

By far the most perplexing aspect of the Hammersteiner divorce is the question of motive. Why would Henry II or the archbishop of Mainz be so insistent that the marriage be annulled. The sources are very obscure on this point. There is reference only to the couple's close relationship, but no details are given. It is of course precisely this fact that sends scholars searching for the genealogical details. When these were discovered in the *vita*[205] and the Seligenstadt[206] canons, the mystery deepened. For it turned out (the most recent investigations are very thorough) that Otto and Irmingard were related in the seventh degree: Otto's maternal great-grandmother and Irmingard's paternal grandfather were brother and sister and thus Irmingard's father and Otto's grandmother were first cousins.[207] But marriages of this nature were rarely disallowed or even challenged, so that the motive of consanguinity might be a red herring. The true motive for the attack upon the Hammerstein couple must be sought elsewhere.[208]

But on with the tale. Otto, frustrated at every angle and reluctant to leave his wife, took one final desperate gamble. In the summer of 1020, he attempted to kidnap the archbishop in order to force that cleric to change his mind. But the attempt failed, and Erkenbald escaped unharmed.[209] Now Henry II moved with great energy against the count. In September 1020 he assembled an army before the castle of the Hammerstein where the couple had gone to seek refuge. It took four months to starve the garrison into surrender. On 26 December 1020, St. Stephen's Day, Otto and Irmingard surrendered in return for free passage out of the fortress.[210] The emperor burned down the castle and the loving couple lived the next two years in poverty, excommunicated and outlawed, strangers in their own land.

This might have been the end of the story, had not the situation changed radically in 1021. Archbishop Erkenbald died and Aribo, a cleric from Bavaria and a friend of the emperor, took his place. At the same time there was also a new archbishop in Cologne, one Pilgrim, another Bavarian. Both men were relatively young and came from the same milieu, but there the similarities ended. Aribo was an "old-style" churchman—jealous of his prerogatives as a bishop, harsh of personality, conservative in his views on marriage, and anti-papal in his political stance.[211] Pilgrim, on the other hand, was more progressive in his ideas on church practices, an intellectual, kind and pleasant, interested in reform and more conciliatory towards the papacy.[212] Both men had jurisdiction over the Hammerstein matter: Aribo, because the county of the Wetterau lay within the Mainz diocese; Pilgrim because the Hammerstein and Irmingard's connections were with Cologne.

Some time before 1023, Otto of Hammerstein attempted to resolve the matter of his marriage and his lands with the new archbishop. But Aribo proved immovable. He demanded that Otto leave his wife permanently if he ever wanted to be reinstated in his possessions. Otto seemed to comply and he returned to his status as count of the Wetterau.[213]

Irmingard, however, refused to abide by Aribo's demands. For some time now she resided in or near Cologne (or perhaps at Vilich) and she consulted with Archbishop Pilgrim. He recommended that she appeal her case to Pope Benedict VIII for a ruling. It has, in fact, been conjectured that the discrepancy between Otto's and Irmingard's actions regarding their marriage was the result of a joint plan, although there is no direct evidence of this. In any event, Irmingard went to Rome in the company of Pilgrim, who was on his way there to receive the pallium, and placed the matter before the pontiff.[214] A record of her interview with Benedict is not extant, but the case became the touchstone of a bitter feud between Mainz and Rome over final jurisdiction in matters regarding the German church. The dispute ended only with the deaths of the Pope in 1024 and the emperor Henry II shortly after. Otto and Irmingard reunited after her return from Rome and their marriage was protected from any further clerical attempts to disrupt it by the favour of the new ruler, Conrad II, who honoured the couple as his close relatives.[215] The death of their only son in 1034 was followed by Otto's demise in 1036.[216] Irmingard died sometime before 1042.[217]

Appendix

A Latin Chapter of the *Vita:* Notes on the History of an Historical Document

THE PRIMARY INTENT OF THE PRECEDING CHAPTERS HAS been to translate into English a significant historical document and to explore the various social, political, and religious ideas that arise from it. For an proper understanding of this *vita,* however, it also important to outline the manuscript tradition, its literary background, and the location of the extant manuscripts.

The *Vita Adelheidis* was written in Latin rhymed prose[218] which the author may have used in preference to prose alone because it reminded her of the rhyme schemes of her native tongue. The excerpt which follows from Chapter Ten is an attempt to reveal the rhyme scheme which lies behind the prose of the *vita.*

Dehinc magis ac magis ubivis
crescente signorum fama,
illo tendens omnis qui vel egritudinis
vel alicuius molestiœ laborat plaga,
quasi certissimum suœ liberationis
confugium frequentare non cessaverant tumulum.
Inter quos venerat quidam nobilis,
pro penitentia cuiusdam criminis
ferreis nexibus apostolica auctoritate ligatus;
a quibus post multa sanctorum perlustrata
limina inibi tandem meritis
illius ita evidenter est relaxatus,
ut dissolutorum proculque dissilientium
vinculorum tinnitus
omnium tunc in monasterio consistentium
perculisset auditus.
Veneranda igitur abbatissa
materterœ suœ docta pietate,
hunc absolutum per aliquantum temporis
magnœ humanitatis tractabat
officio una cum germano fratre,
qui proximum tanquam se ipsum
diligens caritate non ficta,
licet innocens, exceptis vinculis,
per omnia communicato labore fratris emendavit delicta.
Cumque, adhibito sibi tantœ pietatis fomento,
emortuœ manus vel brachia pristini vigoris
reviviscerent incremento,
adiutos caballis vel vestimentis
repatriare permisit magna hilaritate mentis.
Ad vincula etiam sancti Petri,
nostri scilicet spetialis patroni,
cuius hoc cenobium dicatum est honori,
quidam paraliticus,
autium vel oculorum officio privatus,
ad sacrœ virginis tumbam sanitati est donatus.[219]

This story of the unknown nobleman who committed some unknown crime and was rescued by the intervention of the saint presents some of Bertha's finest qualities as a writer. High seriousness and a sense of drama are juxtaposed with a great gift for appreciating the practical problems of everyday existence. Although the saint was the instrument through which God worked his miracles, it was the abbess, the niece of the saint, whose care revived the numbed arms and legs and who provided the clothes and horses so that the two young men could return to their home.[220]

The *Vita Adelheidis* was written about 1057, a date inferred from internal evidence which speaks of the recent death of the emperor Henry III who died in 1056.[221] Little is known about the author or the methods she used to research her story.[222] Archæological evidence and other documents, however, have more than substantiated her version of Adelheid's life.

Bertha's excellent education and fluent Latin style is generally recognised. Interestingly enough, the only text she quotes is the Bible which she uses extensively, sometimes only allusively, sometimes quoting directly and with good effect. Often Biblical references are reworded so that they might fit into her rhymed prose pattern.[223]

The *Vita Adelheidis* has been preserved in two separate manuscripts. In both, the text of the *vita* forms part of a larger legendary produced in the Rhineland in the late twelfth or early thirteenth century. Arranged in calendar form, the saints whose lives have been included all predate 1100.[224] Many are from the formative years of the Christian era and most were active as missionaries in northern France, Belgium, the Netherlands and northern Germany. A few formed the nucleus of a local cult, such as Adelheid of Vilich and Heribert of Cologne.[225]

This English translation of the *Vita Adelheidis* is based on the printed edition published in 1887/1888 by the *Monu-*

menta Germaniæ Historica, Scriptorum VX. Its editor, D. Holder-Egger, made use of Brussels Bibliothèque Royale MS 98-100, a three-volume legendary which bears the seal of the Bibliothèque Nationale in Paris and may have been brought to Paris by French revolutionary forces about 1794. In 1815 the volumes were given to Belgium as compensation for the loss of manuscripts in the Napoleonic wars. The provenance of these volumes is uncertain. It is probable that they came from the Cologne area, perhaps at the Premonstratensian abbey of Knechtsteden. The three volumes were listed in the 1748 edition of the catalogue of the Carthusian monastery of St. Barbara in Cologne, but they could not have been produced there since the manuscript dates from the thirteenth century and the abbey itself was founded in 1335. In November 1451, a fire destroyed its library and it may be conjectured that the MS was bought at that time to replace those volumes which had been burned. Presumably it was this manuscript which Laurentius Surius used as the basis of the *Vita Adelheidis* which is found in his *De probatis sanctorum historiis.*[227] The *vita* can also be found in the *Acta Sanctorum,* 1 February, edited by Johannes Bollandus, a version which Jean Mabillon reproduced somewhat later in the *Acta sanctorum ordinis S. Benedicti.*[228]

The second manuscript which contains the *Vita Adelheidis,* British Library, Harl. 2800, 2801, 2802, dates from the first decade of the thirteenth century. Produced at the monastery of Arnstein in Nassau, it remained there until 1720 when Robert Harley, Earl of Oxford, acquired it and brought the three volumes to London. The pages are arranged in two columns with large initials, some decorations, and few representations of the saints. In Volume 1, where the *Vita Adelheidis* is found, there are only thirteen initials with figures out of a total of 262 pages. Adelheid is only saint who is identified by name. This manuscript was not used by Holder-Egger for his *Monumenta* edition, but from the investigations of Levison and, more recently, Maurice Coens,[230] it appears that both the Brussels and the London MSS arose from a common source, possibly a legendary from the Rhineland area in the twelfth century. It is tempting to speculate that the place of origin of the *Vita Adelheidis,* at least, might have been Brauweiler for Bertha writes that she had sent a copy of it to her brother, Abbot Wolfhelm.

The Ancestors and Family of Adelheid of Vilich

Genealogical Tables

Kings of France and Germany in capitals
References to tables in Roman numerals

Abbreviations:

A. Archbishop   B. Bishop
Ab. Abbess   C. Count
D. Duke   Q. Queen
P. Pope   s. son
d. daughter   dotted lines: illegitimate line

Table I
The Late Carolingians

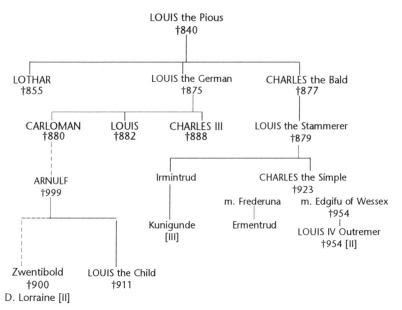

Table II.
The Saxon/Ottonian Royal House

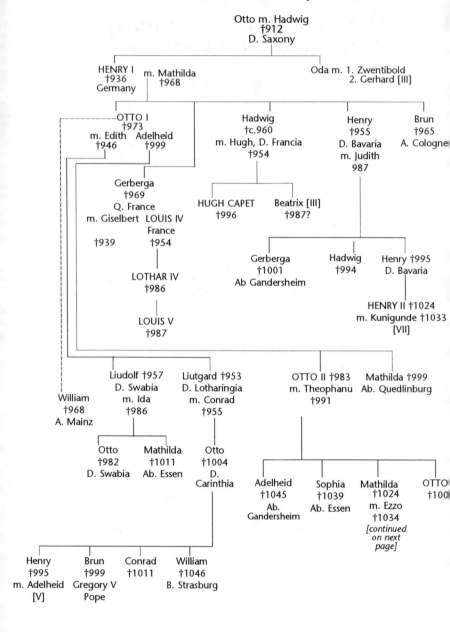

Table II.
The Saxon/Ottonian Royal House
(continued)

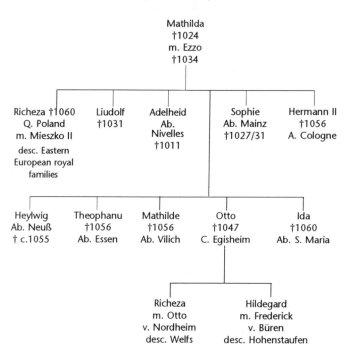

Mathilda
†1024
m. Ezzo
†1034

| Richeza †1060 Q. Poland m. Mieszko II desc. Eastern European royal families | Liudolf †1031 | Adelheid Ab. Nivelles †1011 | Sophie Ab. Mainz †1027/31 | Hermann II †1056 A. Cologne |

| Heylwig Ab. Neuß † c.1055 | Theophanu †1056 Ab. Essen | Mathilde †1056 Ab. Vilich | Otto †1047 C. Egisheim | Ida †1060 Ab. S. Maria |

Richeza
m. Otto
v. Nordheim
desc. Welfs

Hildegard
m. Frederick
v. Büren
desc. Hohenstaufen

Table III.
The Ancestors of the Vilich Founders

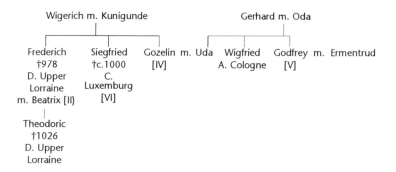

Wigerich m. Kunigunde

Gerhard m. Oda

| Frederich †978 D. Upper Lorraine m. Beatrix [II] | Siegfried †c.1000 C. Luxemburg [VI] | Gozelin m. Uda [IV] | Wigfried A. Cologne | Godfrey m. Ermentrud [V] |

Theodoric
†1026
D. Upper
Lorraine

Table IV.
Family of Irmingard of Hammerstein

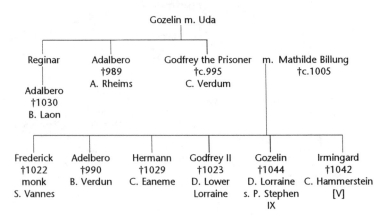

Table V.
The Vilich Family

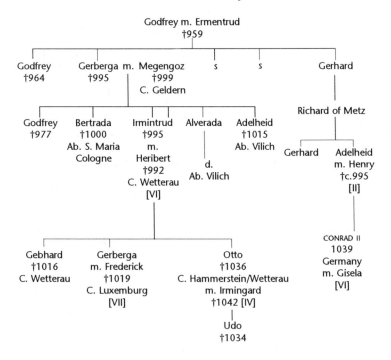

Table VI.
The Conradin Family

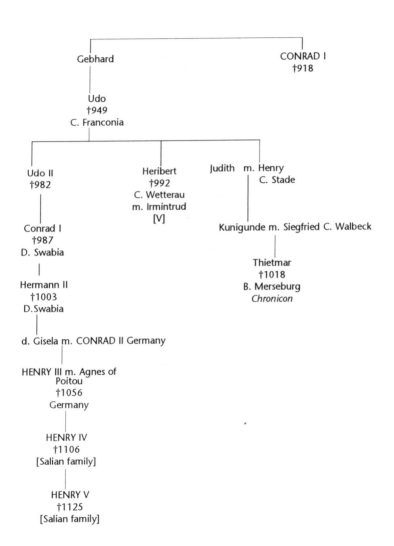

Table VII.
The Luxemburg Family

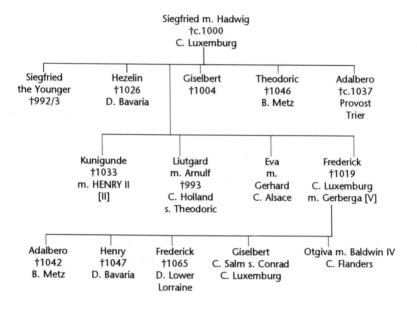

Siegfried m. Hadwig
†c.1000
C. Luxemburg

Siegfried the Younger †992/3	Hezelin †1026 D. Bavaria	Giselbert †1004	Theodoric †1046 B. Metz	Adalbero †c.1037 Provost Trier

Kunigunde †1033 m. HENRY II [II]	Liutgard m. Arnulf †993 C. Holland s. Theodoric	Eva m. Gerhard C. Alsace	Frederick †1019 C. Luxemburg m. Gerberga [V]

Adalbero †1042 B. Metz	Henry †1047 D. Bavaria	Frederick †1065 D. Lower Lorraine	Giselbert C. Salm s. Conrad C. Luxemburg	Otgiva m. Baldwin IV C. Flanders

End Notes

CHAPTER ONE:

THE SOURCE

1.   Implied here are terms of equality: *Comfortata exemplo Abrahæ patriarchæ Deum familiari allocutione sepius convenire audentis . . . .*

2.   Ps 113. Indirect biblical quotations are translated as part of the text of the *vita.* Direct quotations are given in the English of the *Revised Standard Version of the Bible.*

3.   Mt 6:30; 14:31.

4.   Mt 7:3; 12:1–8.

5.   The Latin is *cubicularia,* the feminine form of *cubicularius,* a chamberlain, the servant who waited upon her in her bedroom.

6.   *Quod mea adhoc opus . . . incipientia:* "that my wisdom could never have sought to rise to this work" or, in more colloquial usage, "that my work would never have got off the ground" (Irmingard Achter, *Die Siftskirche St. Peter in Vilich,* Die Kunstdenkmaler des Rheinlandes 52 (Düsseldorf: Rheinland Verlag, 1968), p. 267.

7.   Bertha sent her manuscript to her brother Wolfhelm at Brauweiler for revisions. See Chapter 2.

8.   Jn 3:8.

9.   1 Cor 12:6.

10.   See the genealogical tables for the widespread connections of the Vilich family.

11. References to the Rule here and elsewhere apply to Benedict of Nursia whose sixth-century *regula* was the basic order

order of monastic life in the early Middle Ages: *RB 1980: The Rule of St. Benedict in Latin and English,* with Notes, ed. Timothy Fry (Collegeville MN; The Liturgical Press, 1981).

12.   Jerome did not actually write a rule, but his advice to his women friends on Christian living and education was incorporated into the *Institutio sanctimonialium* of the council of Aachen of 816. Bertha most probably read what Jerome had to say about Christian life in this source, for it is far more likely that the Vilich library contained a copy of the *Inst. sanct.* than a copy of the letters of Jerome. See Chapter 3 and n. 96.

13.   Wis 4:8.

14.   1 Cor 7:31.

15.   Jas 1:22.

16.   1 Tim 5:3–16.

17.   Lk 12:42.

18.   Adelheid was encouraged by her mother to follow the Rule of Benedict rather than the less strict conventual life laid down by the *Institutio sanctimonialium.* For a discussion of this issue as it relates to Vilich, see Chapters 3 and 4.

19.   *Et qualiter ad monachicam religionem . . . .* The term *religio* is an important one. *The Oxford English Dictionary* gives the following etymology: "AF. *religiun* (11th c.), F. *religion,* or ad. L. *religio<um>n-em,* of doubtful etymology; by Cicero connected with *relege<ang>re* to read over again, but by later authors with *religa<um>re* to bind, religate. See Lewis and Short, s.v.); the latter view has usually been favoured by modern writers in explaining the force of the word by its supposed etymological meaning." In the context of the *Vita Adelheidis,* it means "the recognition on the part [of the saint] of some higher unseen power as having control of [her] destiny, and as being entitled to obedience, reverence, and worship; the general mental and moral attitude resulting from this belief, with reference to its effect upon the individual or the community; personal or general acceptance of this feeling as a standard of spiritual and practical life" (OED).

20.   Lk 14:30.

21.   1 Cor 7:7.

22.   The ideas expressed here repeat the *Inst. sanct.* of Aachen, 816. See Chapter 3.

23.   2 Tim 4:2.

24.   Is 57:1.

25.   Lk 12:31.

26.   See *Inst. sanct.* XVII.

27.   Quarter-days are the dates at which tenancies begin or end and when quarterly rents are due: Lady Day (25 March); Midsummer Day (24 June); Michaelmas (29 September) and Christmas (25 December) or sometimes Candlemas (2 February); Whitsunday (15 May); Lammas (1 August) and Martinmas (11 November); 1 January; 1 April; 1 July; and 1 October. Quarterly payments today are collected on 1 January, 1 April, 1 July and 1 October.

28.   For Adelheid's work with famine relief, see Chapter 4.

29.   Mt 25:29.

30.   Mt 25:21

31.   Lk 12:48.

32.   1 Cor 3:2; 1 Pet 2:2.

33.   Mt 6:4.

34.   1 Cor 7:7.

35.   Phil 2:12.; Lk 17:10.

36.   Mt 5:15.

37.   Mt 6:18; 16:27.

38.   2 Cor 12:9.

39.   February 3.

40. February 5, the feastday of St. Agatha, has also tradition-ally been the feastday of Adelheid. It was possibly the day the nuns took her body to Vilich and interred it in the cloister.

41. Lk 1:48.

42. Lk 14:10.

CHAPTER TWO:

WOMEN OF POWER

43. For a biography of Bertha, see below. For some comments on her authorship as well as some notes on the manuscript tradi-tions and editions, see Appendix.

44. See Chapter 5 for the full details.

45. Investigations into the family of the Vilich founders as well as the Hammerstein connection have continued ever since Harry Bresslau opened the issue in the third volume of the *Jahrbücher des deutschen Reiches unter Heinrich II* and took the matter up again in "Otto von Hammerstein und sein Haus": Siegfried Hirsch, *Jahrbücher des deutschen Reiches unter Heinrich II*, 3 vols. Ed. Harry Bresslau (Berlin: Duncker and Humblot, 1862–1875); "Otto von Hammerstein und sein Haus" *Forschungen zur deutschen Geschichte 21 (1881): pp. 40. See also Dorothea von Kessler, Der Eheprozess Ottos und Irmingards von Hammerstein,* Ebering's Historische Studien 157 (Berlin: Ebering, 1923). More recently see Eduard Hlawitschka, *Die Anfänge des Hauses Habsburg-Lothringen und des Reiches im 9. und 10. Jahr-hundert* (Saarbrucken: Minerva Verlag, 1969) and Siegfried Reicke, "Der Hammersteiner Ehehandel im Lichte der mittel-älterlichen Herrschaftsordnung," ed. Ursula Lewald *Rheinische Vierteljahresblätter* 38 (1974): 203–224.

46. See Helmut Diwalt: "In this connection [referring to a previous discussion of women, their beauty, and their ability, in various literary sources], a particularly important sign appears to be the self-conscious position of the woman in society, the

certainty and strength of her presentation. The difference to later periods is so startling, that the tenth century in Germany should be called a century of women" [Helmut Diwalt, *Heinrich der Erste* (Bergisch Gladbach: Gustav Lubbe Verlag, 1987), pp. 356–357].

47.   In the *vita*, Bertha calls Godfrey (in German, Gottfried) a duke, but that is a usage more common to her times. There was no duke called Godfrey in Lotharingia in the early tenth century.

48.   See *Vita Brunonis* c. 41 in Hatto Kallfelz, *Lebensbeschreibungen einiger Bischofe des 10. bis 12. Jahrhundert* (Darmstadt: Wissenschaftliche Buchgesellschaft, 1973): pp. 242–243. The death of young Godfrey occurred in July, 964.

49.   The relationship comes through Adelheid, the wife of Henry of Speyer, the mother of Conrad II, the first Salian ruler, and grandmother of Henry III. Adelheid's father and thus her descent from one of Gerberga's brothers is not entirely certain. See Hlawitschka, *Die Anfänge des Hauses Habsburg-Lothringen,* pp. 67ff. See also Tilman Schmidt, "Kaiser Konrad II. Jugend und Familie" *Geschichtsschreibung und gesistiges Leben. Festschrift Heinz Lowe* (Köln: Bohlau, 1978), pp. 312–324 and Wipo, "Vita Conradis" in Theodor Ernst Mommsen and Carl Morrison. *Imperial Lives and Letters of the Eleventh Century* (New York: Columbia University Press, 1962).

50.   For the canons of Seligenstadt see *M.G.h. Constitutiones* I, p. 639. See also *Jahrbücher des deutschen Reiches unter Heinrich II,* Vol. III, pp. 267ff; 349ff.

51.   Oda's first marriage had been to Zwentibold, Duke of Lotharingia, the illegitimate son of the Emperor Arnulf (†899) and half-brother of Louis the Child, the last Carolingian ruler of the East Frankish realm [i.e. Germany]. See Robert Holtzmann, *Geschichte der sächsischen Kaiserzeit* (1941; rpt. München: Verlag Georg D. W. Callway, 1961): pp. 41–42 and the Genealogical Table in this study.

52.   See M.G.h. DOI, 59. Aug. 944. See also Theodor Lacomblet, *Urkundenbuch für die Geschichte des Niederrheins* I, 96 (1840; rpt. Aalen: Scientia Verlag, 1960): p. 53.

53.   One of the most difficult jobs for the mediæval historian is the accurate dating of people's lives. The death dates of famous men are usually recorded, much less frequently than their birth dates, except of course if they were the sons of kings whose arrival had been eagerly awaited. The death dates of well-known women were also usually recorded, although the birth date is often not available. When the person is less well-placed, the task becomes almost impossible. It is not always safe to assume that women married in their early teens and, furthermore, consideration has to be given to the age at which women gave birth. It is rare even today for women to give birth in their late forties and early fifties, a fact which genealogists have often overlooked. The birth and death dates given here have been taken from available sources, as well as from numerous scholarly studies, the latest being Hlawitschka, *Die Anfänge des Hauses Habsburg-Lothringen.*

54.   Reference to Gebhard's death is in Thietmar, *Chronicon,* 7, 49: Thietmar von Merseburg, *Chronik,* trans. Werner Trillman (Berlin: Deutscher Verlag der Wissenschaften, 1966).

55.   The name of the sister of Otto of Hammerstein is uncertain, but Gerberga, her grandmother's name, seems a logical choice.

56.   For a discussion of the information relating to the Vilich founders and their family see, for instance, E. Kempen, "Rheinische Anfänge des Hauses Habsburg-Lothringen" *Annalen des Historischen Vereins für den Niederrhein* 23 (1933), pp. 22ff. and Erich Wisplinhoff, "Zur Frühgeschichte von Vilich" *Rheinische Vierteljahrblatter* 18 (1953): pp. 78–83.

57.   The story of Adelheid is detailed in Chapter 4.

58.   See *Vita Mahtilda antiquior, M.G.h.* SS X, pp. 573–582; *Vita Mahtilda posterior, M.G.h.* SS IV, pp. 282–302; Wilhelm Wattenbach and Robert Holtzmann, *Deutschland's Geschichtsquellen im Mittelalter:* Vol. 1, 3: *Die Zeit der Sachsen und Salier,* ed. Franz Josef Schmale (Köln: Bohlaus Verlag, 1967); *Jahrbücher des deutschen Reiches unter Otto I* and Diwalt, *Heinrich der Erste.*

59.   *Odilonis Cluniacensis abbatis Epitaphium domine Adelheide auguste, M.G.h.* SS IV, pp. 636–649. A book containing

an English translation of Odilo's work and a study of Adelheid's life is in progress by the author under the title *Domina regnorum.*

60. Wimmer, Franz Paul, *Kaiserin Adelheid, Gemahlin Ottos I des Grossen in ihrem Leben und Wirken von 931–973* (Regensburg: J. Habbel, 1897); Gertrud Bäumer, *Otto I und Adelheid: Adelheid, Mutter der Königreiche* (Tübingen und Stuttgart: Rainer Wunderlich Verlag, 1951): a novel; and Dick, "The Empress Adelheid: A Portrait Study from the Tenth Century."

61. Liudprand of Cremona's embassy to Constantinople is related in *Liudprandi Legatio ad Imperatorem Constantinopolitanum Nicephorum Phocam* in *Quellen zur Geschichte der sächsischen Kaiserzeit,* ed. Albert Bauer and Reinhold Bau (Darmstadt: Wissenschaftliche Buchgesellschaft, 1971), pp. 518–589 and in J.D. Sutherland, "The Mission of Liudprand of Cremona" *Traditio* 31 (1975): pp. 55–81.

62. Gunther Wolf has reopened the question of Theophanu's relationship to John Tzimisces. He proposes that she was related to his first wife, Maria Sclereina who died before 967, and thus was undoubtedly his niece, as was reported. Wolf argues that Theophanu was the daughter of Constantine Sclerus (†991), a brother of Maria, and Sophia Phocaina, a niece of the Emperor Nicephorus II Phocas (†969). These connections are not "imperial" in the strictest sense of the word but they certainly were of high noble status. One of the "proofs" of this thesis is the use of the name "Sophia" for Theophanu's second daughter. Wolf argues for a scheme in the naming of the children: paternal family names and maternal family name alternating. The name Sophia comes to the Ottonian scheme after Theophanu's arrival. See *Kaiserin Theophanu: Prinzessin aus der Fremde des Westreiches Große Kaiserin,* ed. Gunther Wolf et al. (Köln: Böhlau Verlag, 1991), pp. 58–59, esp. p. 67, 70–71, 168–199).

63. For the history of the empire under Theophanu see *Jahrbücher unter Otto II,* Holtzmann, *Sächsische Kaiserzeit* and Helmut Hiller, *Otto der Grosse und seine Zeit* (München: List Verlag, 1980).

64. In a letter dated 17 December 983, ten days after Otto II died of of typhus in Rome, Gerbert wrote from Bobbio (a

monastery in Italy where, at the time, he was a rather unsuccessful abbot) to Pope John XIV about his troubles and then went on: "We love Lady Imiza because she loves you. Let us know through her, either by messengers or by letters, whatever you wish us to do, while at the same time, through her, we shall inform you of anything that concerns you relative to the condition and undertakings of the kingdom" (*Sylvester II: The Letters of Gerbert of Aurillac,* trans. Harriet Pratt Lattin (New York: Columbia University Press, 1961), Letter 21, pp. 59–60.

65. Sylvester II; *Letters of Gerbert of Aurillac,* Letter 30, pp. 67–68. It does not take much probing to discover to what Gerbert was so succinctly referring, for the events of the spring and summer of 984 were among the most tumultous in the annals of the Ottonian family saga. In 983, after Otto II's premature death, his widow was in Rome, while the new king, Otto III, a child of four, was in Germany. Henry of Bavaria, in an attempt to wrest the crown from his cousin's son, had "kidnapped" the child and held him hostage in Saxony throughout the winter. It was not until mid-984 that Theophanu was reunited with her son, established firmly as his regent, and was able to deal with the threat of Henry of Bavaria. See *Jahrbücher des deutschen Reiches unter Otto II und Otto III,* Vol. 2, 35ff.

66. The *Colloquium dominarum* was a meeting of highly placed ladies who came together to consult about the problems of the frontier between Germany and France. In March 985, the young king Lothar IV had attacked the fortress and town of Verdun and taken prisoner its count, Godfrey. Godfrey's disappearance brought much anxiety to the region, especially in Rheims where his uncle was the Archbishop. See *Jahrbücher unter Otto II und Otto III,* Vol. 2, p. 54. See also Sylvester II, Letter 68, pp. 109–110; Letter 69, p. 110; Letter 72, p. 112; and Madelyn Bergen Dick, "*Colloquium dominarum:* Political Activity of Aristocratic Women in Ottonian Germany." Paper presented at the 23rd International Congress of Medieval Studies, the Medieval Institute, Western Michigan University, Kalamazoo, Michigan, 7 May, 1988.

67. The story of Theophanu has fascinated many and the debate about her origins has not yet ended. See Thietmar of

Merseburg, *Chronicon* II, c. 15ff., and his modern interpreters such as Uhlriz who suggested that Theophanu could be the daughter of the Caesar Stephanos Lecapenos and the Augusta Anna [Mathilda Uhlirz, "Studien über Theophanu: I und II" *Deutsches Archiv* 6 (1943), pp. 442–474]. More recently, in *Kaiserin Theophanu*, Wolf has reopened the question by examining Theophanu's relationship to the Emperor John Tzimisces. See n. 62 above. There is no biography of Theopanu, either mediæval or modern, although Wolf's collected studies commemorate the 1000th anniversary of her death is very complete. See also Rosamond McKitterick, "Ottonian Intellectual Culture in the Tenth Century and the Role of Theophanu," *Early Medieval History* 2 (1993): 53–74.

68.   See *M.G.h.* DHII, no. 409, dated May 20, 1019. " . . . qui in Christo sumus una caro." and in Kunigunde's own charter in 1025 (p. 698) " . . . sui vero mariti." See also *Jahrbücher des deutschen Reiches unter Heinrich II,* Vol. III, pp. 359–361 and Hans Leo Mikoletzky, *Kaiser Heinrich II und die Kirche (*Wien: Universum, 1946). The legends about Henry II and Kunigunde originated with the canonisation of Henry II by Eugenius III on March 14, 1146; see *M.G.h.* SS IV, pp. 679–828.

69.   Kunigunde's canonisation was performed by Innocent III on April 3, 1200 upon the request of the Bamberg episcopal church, which had originated in the time of his predecessor Lucius III. It involved the story of her chaste marriage and her trial by the ordeal of fire. Both these stories are quite possibly of later origin and have to be regarded with some caution. The author is indebted to Professor John W. Baldwin for his remarks during the Bertie Wilkinson lecture, 22 January 1993 entitled "The Crisis of the Ordeal: Literature, Law and Religion around 1200."

70.   For the contemporary accounts of Kunigunde's life, see Thietmar, *Chronicon,* IV. V, VI, VII, VIII. See also *Jahrbücher unter Heinrich II,* Vol. 1, pp. 184; 225; 301; 307; Vol. 2, 334ff.; Vol. 3, 55; 73ff.; 117; 158; 234; 359–361. See also Holtzmann, *Geschichte des sächsischen Kaiserzeit,* pp. 390–522.

71.   Albert Groeteken postulated that this abbess was still alive when Bertha came to Vilich to write the *vita.* This seems a bit

improbable, since Adelheid died in 1015 and Bertha did not write her book until 1056–1057, at which date Vilich was headed by the third abbess, Mathilda (*Die Heilige Adelheid von Vilich und ihre Familie* (Kevelaer: Verlag Butzon und Bercker, 1937), p. 20).

72. See Ursula Lewald, "Die Ezzonen" *Rheinische Vierteljahrblatter: Mitteilungen für Geschichtliche Landeskunde des Rheinlandes an der Universität Bonn* 43 (1979), pp. 120–168. Lewald's major primary source was *Fundatio Brunwilarensis monasterii*, the story of the foundation of the monastery of Brauweiler which was begun on April 14, 1024, the monastery being dedicated on November 8, 1028. The *Fundatio* was written between 1063 and 1080 and dedicated to Wolfhelm, the Abbot of Brauweiler, who was the brother of Bertha, the author of the Vilich *vita*. For the older scholarship, including some comments on the usefulness of the *Fundatio*, see R. Usingen, "Pfalzgraf Ezzo" (Excursus IV) *Jahrbücher des deutschen Reiches unter Heinrich II*, pp. 447–454. See also Wattenbach-Holtzmann, *Geschichtsquellen*, Vol. 2, pp. 644–645.

73. Ezzo is the usual name for this noble from the Lotharingian frontier, but elsewhere his name is recorded as Erenfried. See Lacomblet, *Urkundenbuch*, Vol. 1, 164, p. 102. The tenth and early eleventh centuries seem to have been fond of nicknames often with z-sounds, i.e., Irmintrud becomes Imiza, Henry Hezelin and Erenfried Ezzo.

74. Thietmar of Merseburg, *Chronicon*, IV, 60, pp. 177.

75. Thietmar, *Chronicon*, IV, 60. reports that the marriage was regarded by contemporaries as a mesalliance, but that Otto III, the bride's brother, gave his consent *legaliter*, alluding perhaps to a contract or obligation, and gave lands and riches to his new brother-in-law: "Cesaris eiusdem soror Mahtild nomine Herimanni comitis palatini filio Ezoni nupsit. Et hoc multos displicuit. Sed quia id non valuit emendare legaliter frater illius pacienter, dans ei quam plurima ne vilesceret innate sibi parentibus summis gloria." See *Fundatio* c. 6. in Herman Pabst, "Brauweiler Geschichtsquellen" *Archiv der Gesellschaft für altere deutsche Geschichtskunde* 12 (1858–1874), pp. 158–159.

76. For the throne feud of 1002, see *Jahrbücher des deutschen*

Reiches unter Heinrich II, Vol. I, pp. 193–242 and Holtzmann, *Sächsische Kaiserzeit,* pp. 383–395.

77. Beatrice of Lotharingia was a daughter of Hugh the Great Count of Paris and his wife Hadwig, daughter of Henry I of Germany, and thus sister of Hugh Capet. She disappeared from the sources about 987 either through death or an obscure late marriage. Her relations with her son were not good.

78. The future Conrad II. See the *vita* by Wipo in Mommson and Morrison, eds. *Imperial Lives and Letters,* pp. 52–99.

79. In *Kaiserin Theophanu,* Wolf reexamines the fate of the house of Ezzo (pp. 180–199). See also the Genealogical Table in this study.

80. See Lacomblet, *Urkundenbuch,* no. 244, p. 157. In 1090, Hermann III settled the dispute over Clotten in Brauweiler's favour. See also Georg Jenal, *Erzbischof Anno II von Köln (1056–1075) und sein politisches Werken.* 2 vols. (Stuttgart: Anton Hiersemann, 1974).

81. Vilich did not fall under the control of Cologne until 1291. See Chapter 3.

82. See K.J. Leyser, *Rule and Conflict in an Early Medieval Society: Ottonian Saxony* (Bloomington: Indiana University Press, 1979), pp. 49–62.

83. See Lewald, "Irmgard von Hammerstein," *Neue Biographie* 10, pp. 180–181 for the sources and discussions of the life of Irmingard.

84. See Hlawitschka, "Gottfried der Gefangene, Graf von Verdun," *Neue Biographie* 6, pp. 666–667 for a review of the story of Godfrey.

85. The question of the Hammersteiner children has been part of the investigation of the Hammersteiner divorce. For decades scholars sought to associate the family and particularly Irmingard and a possible daughter to the monastery of Rees, mainly because a countess by that name turned up in the charters of Henry III. However, in a masterful article, first published in 1949, Oediger put that theory quite firmly into the realm of

impossibility: Friedrich Wilhelm Oediger, "Die Anfänge des Stiftes Rees und die Gräfin[nen] Irmingardis [und Irmintrudis] von Aspel" in *Vom Leben am Niederrhein* (Düsseldorf: Pädagogischer Verlag Schwann, 1973), pp. 236–249.

86. For the battle at the Ungarnberg in the upper Brenna pass (near Verona) see Thietmar, *Chronicon*, V, 24–26; *Jahrbücher des deutschen Reiches unter Heinrich II*, Vol. 1, pp. 240 242; Holtzmann, *Sächsische Kaiserzeit*, pp. 401–402. Otto of Hammerstein was second-in-command to Otto of Carinthia, son of Conrad the Red and Liutgard the eldest daughter of Otto I, and thus the grandfather of the emperor Conrad II and founder of the Salian royal family. The fact that Duke Otto and the imperial army lost the battle endeared neither him nor the young soldier to the emperor Henry II, who had just won his crown as successor of his cousin Otto III and in opposition to the same duke who had also wished to become king. It is quite possible that Otto of Hammerstein's own connection to the older line of the Conradin family, through his father, and his connection to Otto of Worms through his grandmother was also a factor in Henry II's abiding dislike of him, a dislike that was certainly evident in his attack on the Hammersteiner marriage. For a somewhat embellished discussion of Henry II's character and his ideas on the empire, see Wilhelm von Giesebrecht, *Geschichte der deutschen Kaiserzeit* 2 (Braunschweig: Schwetschke, 1881), pp. 1–205.

87. In the canons of the synod of Seligenstadt, Irmingard's refusal to recognise the divorce of her marriage occasioned some harsh words from the clerical recorder. There is also a letter from the suffragan bishops of the Archdiocese of Mainz from 1024 to Benedict VIII objecting to his actions in this matter. See Giesebrecht, *Geschichte der deutsche Kaiserzeit 2*, p. 693 and Chapter 5.

88. *Vita Wolfhelmi c. 25. M.G.h.* SS XII, p. 190: "Exstisterunt, ait, huic beatissimo viro (Wolfhelmo) . . . sorores sanctimoniales duæ, quaram . . . altera vero Berta nuncupata, litterarum pluremum emicuit scientia. Hæc vitam beatæ Adelheidis, primæ Vilecensis abbatissæ, eleganti satis admodum stilo conscriptis et plurimum religiosis suæ fructum in eodem loco dereliquit."

89. *Vita* c. 2.

CHAPTER THREE:

THE ABBEY

90.   The scholarly literature on these dedicated and spiritually alive women is extensive. Their *vitæ* are being edited and translated and their lives are discussed in books and articles too numerous to mention. See, especially, Jane Tibbetts Schulenburg, "Female Sanctity: Public and Private Roles, ca. 500–1100" in *Women and Power in the Middle Ages*. Ed. Mary Erler and Maryanne Kowaleski (Athens: University of Georgia Press, 1988), pp. 102–125. See also the many studies in *Vox Benedictina: A Journal of Monastic and Feminine Spirituality* (Saskatoon, Toronto: Peregrina Publishing Co., 1984–1994).

91.   See the letters of Paul, especially 1 Tim. 5:3–16; 2 Tim; Philemon; Titus; Eusebius, *History of the Church* and the story of the martyr Perpetua in Peter Dronke, *Women Writers of the Middle Ages: A Critical Study of Texts from Perpetua (†203) to Marguerite Porete (†1310)* (Cambrdige: Cambridge University Press, 1984), pp. 1–35.

92.   *The Letters of St. Jerome,* trans. W.H. Freemantle, with the assistance of G. Lewis and W.G. Martley, A Select Library of Nicene and Post-Nicene Fathers of the Christian Church 6 (Oxford: James Parker; New York: The Christian Literature Company, 1893). The letters are addressed to Paula, Eustochium, Læta, and others.

93.   In German, a canoness is called a *Stiftsfrau,* in Latin *sanctimoniales canonice viventes* or *Deo dicatæ canonice viventes puellæ.* Their convents are called *Stift* in German and, in Latin, *monasterium, monasterium puellæ in quo canonice vivitur, collegium sanctimoniales, congregatio* or *societas.* See K. Heinrich Schäfer, *Die Kanonissenstifter im deutschen Mittelalter* (1907; rpt. Amsterdam: P. Schippers N.V., 1965), pp. 1–69.

94.   See Eleanor S. Duckett, *Anglo-Saxon Saints and Scholars* (Hamden: Archon Books, 1967) and *The Letters of Saint Boniface,* tr. E. Emerton (New York: Octagon Books, 1913).

95.   Some work has been done on individual communities: see, for instance that of Edeltraut Klueting, published in the

series *Germania sacra* [*Das Bistum Osnabrück* (Germania Sacra: Die Bistumer der Kirchenprovinz Koln, N.F. 21), 1986]. Another such series is *Germania monastica* with a number of titles. See also Alois Schröer, *Die Kirche in Westfalen vor der Reformation* (Münster: Aschendorf, 1967).

96.   For a text of the *Institutio sanctimonialium*, see *M.G.h. Leges* III; *Concilia* II, esp. no. 39; *Concilium Aquisgranense* B, pp. 421–455 (cited as *Inst. sanct.*) See also Schäfer, *Kanonissenstifter*, pp. 118–128; Rosamund McKitterick, *The Frankish Kingdoms under the Carolingians* (London: Longman, 1983) pp. 212–13; *Vita*, c. 3. For the Benedictine Rule, see *RB 80: The Rule of St. Benedict in Latin and English*, ed. Timothy Fry et al. (Collegeville MN: The Liturgical Press, 1981), cited as RB). The communities of canonesses may not have followed Benedict to the letter of the Rule, but they did follow the spiritual principles of the Benedictine *vita communis*. Indeed, as the following discussion shows, the communal life of the canonesses did not differ markedly from that of the Benedictine nuns except in the matter of dress and the possible absence of perpetual vows.

97.   See *Inst. sanct.*, p. 423. The *Institutio sanctimoniales* contains twenty-eight chapters on the proper life style of the canonesses. Chapters 1 to 6 and 22 contain long passages from Jerome's letters to Eustochium, Dimetrias, Furia, and Læta, written before 420; Cyprian's third-century "On the Dress of Virgins;" Athanasius's fourth-century "Brides of Christ;" and excerpts from sermons and mention of the sixth-century Rule of Cæsarius of Arles: *The Rule for Nuns of St. Cæsarius of Arles*, trans. Mother Maria Caritas McCarthy (Washington DC: The Catholic University Press, 1960).

98.   When Vilich was founded and the charters were granted to it from the imperial government, it was undoubtedly a house of canonesses. The description of the life-style of its inmates is thus an examination of such a community. However, Adelheid herself made attempts to bring the community under the rule of St. Benedict and Bertha's testimony in the *vita* seems to indicate that she was at least partially successful. In the fourteenth century, Vilich was once again a house of canonesses. See Chap. 4 for a fuller discussion of this puzzle.

99. The *Vita Adelheidis* only indirectly details the life-style of the community at Vilich and the legal documents only describe the immunities. One might assume, however, that the Vilich convent was not so very different from other such houses of canonesses about whom more information—some of it from the later Middle Ages—is available. The main scholarly source is Schäfer, *Kanonissenstifter* although some of his information must be used with care. See also n. 95.

100. The fees for lay advocacy contributed to Vilich's debts in the thirteenth century and eventually forced them to become dependent upon the archbishop of Cologne. On the wealth of canonesses, see Achter, *Stiftskirche,* p. 241 and Schäfer, *Kanonissenstifter,* pp. 205–215 and 263–269.

101. The provisions for the *vita communis* as set down by Benedict in the Rule will be cited at the appropiate places as a means of comparison between two similiar, yet distinct, ways of monastic life.

102. Schäfer, *Kanonissenstifter,* pp. 95–118; RB 60, 62.

103. *Vita,* prologue II.

104. Schäfer, *Kanonissenstifter,* pp. 128–139 on the size of the orders and reception into the ranks of the canonesses; RB, Chapters 58; 59.

105. On schools and the *scholastica,* see Schäfer, *Kanonissenstifter,* pp. 172–179. For an excerpt from Jerome's letter ad Lætam, see *Inst. sanct.* c. XXII: "Ut erga puellas in monasteriis erudiendas magna adhibeatur diligentia." On the requirements of education before full membership, see c. IX "Qualiter his, quæ monasterium expetunt, de rebus propriis suis agendum sit."On the abbess' control over education, see c. XIV "Quod gemina abbatissis sanctimonialibus inpendenda sit pastio."

106. On reception dates and ceremonies, see Schäfer, *Kanonissenstifter,* pp. 139–140. See also pp. 215–220 on the rights of canonesses to return to the world to marry where, on p. 219, there is a reference to the frequency with which the young canonesses from Essen left to marry. One such girl was Princess

Mathilda who left the convent c. 991 to marry Count Ezzo (Ch. 2); RB 5, 6, 7, 58.

107. Schäfer, *Kanonissenstifter*, pp. 140–145; *Inst.sanct.* c. VII "Quales in monasteriis puellaribus debeant esse abbatissæ;" c. XIV; c. XXIV "Quales sint præpositæ constituendæ." The *Epistola ad Oratoriam* of Cæsarius of Arles is quoted at length.

108. The *Vita Adelheidis* makes numerous references to Adelheid's function as a mother figure to her congregation; see, for instance, c. 3. The term *"mater spiritualis"* is found in a charter by Alfrid, Bishop of Hildesheim, which documents the foundation of Essen and adds its constitution. Recorded in 874 at the council of Cologne, this charter was read there by Archbishop Willibert and assented to by the participating bishops. In 947, Essen abbey was badly damaged by fire and many of its early documents were destroyed, but this foundation charter, though damaged, was preserved. Essen's abbess is described as "sanctimonialium congregationem spiritualem matrem," Lacomblet, *Urkundenbuch* I, no. 69. pp. 34–36. Schäfer, *Kanonissenstifter*, p. 143.

109. Schäfer, *Kanonissenstifter*, pp. 146–148.

110. *M.G.h.* DHII 40, Febr. 26, 1003; Achter, *Stiftskirche*, pp. 334–335; RB 64.

111. There is considerable debate as to whether or not such an abbess was a member of the clergy as a deaconess. See Schäfer, *Kanonissenstifter* where he describes the "office" of the deaconess and the associations made in the early Middle Ages between deaconesses and abbesses (pp.1–69). For a modern and much more negative picture, see Aimé Georges Martimort, *Deaconesses: An Historical Study* (San Francisco: Ignatius Press, 1986). Martimort virtually dismisses the clerical nature of the deaconess and sees her importance to western church practice as negligible. In theory, he is probably closer to the evidence than Schäfer, but the reality of practice lies somewhere between these two views. A postscript on the position of women in the modern Catholic church gives ample evidence of Martimort's reluctance to envision a church in which women are granted full clerical status. Although Martimort accuses older scholars of interpreting the evidence too optimisti-

cally, he certainly errs in the opposite direction, since his study is designed to show that women have no place at the altar as priests. See pp. 265–268 for his definition of "clerical."

112. Adelheid's age was between seventeen and twenty-two, while her niece and successor could have been in her thirties. The birth-date of the third abbess, Mathilda, is not known, but her parents married in c. 991 and her mother died in 1025. As Mathilda was abbess possibly as early as the 1030s and died c. 1056, she was born c. 1000 and thus was thirty or more. On the election, inauguration and age of abbesses, see Schäfer, *Kanonissenstifter*, pp. 148–154. Most of Schäfer's references are from the later mediæval centuries and there is very little direct evidence from the tenth and eleventh centuries on this matter. See also Chapter 4.

113. Schäfer, *Kanonissenstifter*, pp. 154–165. See also *Inst. sanct.*, c. VIII "De congregandis in monasterium sanctimonialibus;" RB 3.

114. The Vilich seal is described in Achter, *Stiftskirche*, p. 27. A picture is found on p. 13 [actual size] and, on p. 338, an enlargement. A reproduction of this enlargement is found on p. 98.

115. Schäfer, *Kanonissenstifter*, pp. 166–167; *Inst.sanct.* c. XX "Ut sanctimoniales virorum caveant frequentias" and c. XXIV; RB 65.

116. Schäfer, *Kanonissenstifter*, pp. 167–168. The *decana* is not named in the *Inst. sanct.*, but there is an early English reference in the *Vita S. Liobæ*, quoted in Schäfer. See RB 21.

117. Schäfer, *Kanonissenstifter*, pp. 169–172. Sometimes the abbess held this position in addition to her own duties. In Vilich, Gerberga could be said to have undertaken the duties of the custodian when she supervised the building of Vilich II. In *Vita* c. 3 and 4, Adelheid arranges for the burial of her parents. See RB, Chapters 32, 52.

118. Schools of excellent quality were part of the *raison d'être* for the existence of the communities of canonesses. Herford had such a school, as the "Life of Queen Mathilda" testifies and the convents in Essen and Cologne (the Convent of St. Ursula, some-

times called the Convent of the Holy Virgins) are often mentioned. The best known school was at Gandersheim where students were taught by the learned abbess, Gerberga, and her friend, the dramatist and historian Hrothsvita. See n. 105 above.

119. The *vita* describes several interesting incidents concerning Adelheid's activities in this matter. See Chapters 1 and 4.

120. *Vita* c. 7; Schäfer, *Kanonissenstifter,* pp. 179–182; *Inst. sanct.* c. XXV "Quales constituenda sit cellararia;" RB 31, 35, 48.

121. Schäfer, *Kanonissenstifter,* pp. 179–182; *Inst. sanct.,* c. XXVI "De porta monasterii constituenda;" RB 66.

122. Schäfer, *Kanonissenstifter,* pp. 182–183; *Inst. sanct.,* c. XXI "Ut sanctimoniales erga famulas sibi servientes pervigitem adhibeant custodiam."

123. Schäfer, *Kanonissenstifter,* pp. 183–184; *Inst. sanct.,* c. VII c. X. "Qualiter in monasterio sanctimonialibus conservandum sit.;" c. XIII "Qualiter sanctimoniales stipendia accipere debeant necessaria;" c. XIX "Ut abbatissæ virorum frequentias vitent."

124. Schäfer, *Kanonissenstifter,* pp. 184–188; *Inst. sanct..,* c. XV "Ut ad horas canonicas cælebrandas incunctanter conveniant sanctimoniales;" c. XI "De instantia orationis;" c. XIII "Ut completorium pariter sanctimoniales cælebrent;" RB 8–20. On the canonical hours, see *New Catholic Encyclopedia* Vol. 4, p. 918a. They seem to have been organised by the Council of Aachen in 816 for use in the monastic communities and elsewhere. See also Andrew Hughes, *Medieval Manuscripts for Mass and Office: A Guide to their Organization and Terminology* (Toronto: University of Toronto Press, 1982).

125. *Vita,* c. 7; RB 45.

126. Schäfer, *Kanonissenstifter,* pp. 188–191.

127. Schäfer, *Kanonissenstifter,* pp. 191–203. *Inst. sanct.,* c. X; c. XII "Ut sanctimoniales in una societate viventes æqualiter cibum et potum accipiant;" c. XIII; c. XVII; c. XVIII "Quimodus correptionis erga sanctimoniales delinquentes adhibendus sit;" RB 22.

128. Schäfer, *Kanonissenstifter,* pp. 192–197; *Inst. sanct.,* c. X;

c. XI "Ut monasteria puellarum undeque muniantur et necessaria habitationes interius præparentur;" c. XII; c. XIII; RB 6, 38;
39, 40, 41, 42, 43.

129. No references other than to Adelheid's trips to Cologne
and Aachen are referred to in the *vita*, but the most famous
"vacationers" from convent life were the sisters of Otto III whose
frequent visits at court both in his reign and during the reign of
Henry II caused much clerical displeasure. See Schäfer, *Kanonissenstifter*, pp. 203–205; RB 50; 51; 54; 67.

130. Schäfer, *Kanonissenstifter*, pp. 221–234; *Inst. sanct.*, c. VII;
c. X; c. XIII; c. XVII "Ut nonnisi statuto tempore presbiteri
eorumque ministri monasteria puellarum ingrediantur;" RB 55.
See Cyprian, *De habitu virginum* [The Dress of Virgins].

131. Schäfer discusses the adminstration of the wealth of the
various abbeys (*Kanonissenstifter*, pp. 247–269) into which category charities and hospitals fall (pp. 252–256): *Inst. sanct.*,
c. XXVII "Ut hospitate pauperum extra monasterium sit puellarum;" RB 4.

132. Schäfer, *Kanonissenstifter*, pp. 257–261 and see n. 35. The
existence of a wall is attested to by a single doorway with a late
Romanesque arch which is extant at Vilich: Achter, *Stiftskirche,*
pp. 208–209.

133. Achter is the basis for much of the discussion that follows.
The drawings and sketches of Vilich as it might have looked in
the eleventh century and what the church looks like today were
done by Alison Brown and were based on Achter's architectual
designs and photographs (*Stiftskirche*, pp.135, 137, 165–167, 178,
243, and 10 plates in the appendix).

134. Papal bull of 996, Lacomblet, *Urkundenbuch*, Vol. I, no.
126, p. 77; Achter, *Stiftskirche*, pp. 1–135, 334.

135. Achter, *Stiftskirche*, pp. 135–140. Compare Groeteken, *Die
heilige Adelheid*, pp. 87–97 for a more fanciful version.

136. Achter, *Stiftskirche*, pp. 140–145.

137. For a discussion of Adelheid's cult see *Vita*, c. 8–13 and Chapter 4.

138. Achter, *Stiftskirche*, pp. 145–175.

139. An artist's impression of the internal and external views of Vilich III is found on pp. 68–69.

140. *Ringkrypta* is an architectural term used to describe a semi-circular passage around a tomb which pilgrims used in their veneration: Achter, *Stiftskirche*, pp. 175–179.

141. See *Vita* c. 9.

142. See n. 135.

143. *Vita* c. 7. The charter of Henry II of 26 February 1003 gives Adelheid's name as the abbess of Vilich. " . . . venerabilis eiusdem monasterii abbatissa Adelheyda . . . ." See Chapter 4.

144. *Vita*, c. 9, 10.

145. Achter, *Stiftskirche*, pp. 179–180.

146. "Statutes of Santa Maria," ed. Heinrich Schäfer "Die Statuten von Santa Maria im Kapitol" in "Inventare und Regesten aus den Kölner Pfarrarchiven III," *Annalen des historischen Vereins für den Niederrhein* 70, 76, 58 (1901–1907), pp. 98 ff.

147. Friedrich Wilhelm Oedinger, *Geschichte des Erzbistums Köln I, Das Bistum Koln von den Anfangen bis zum Ende des 12. Jahrhunderts*, 2nd ed. (Köln: Verlag J.P. Bachem, 1972), pp. 399–405.

148. See Chapter 2.

149. Vilich came under the administration of the Archdiocese of Cologne when the archbishop received the advocacy of the cloister on 29 March, 1291. See Achter, *Stiftskirche*, pp. 224–225, 241.

150. Achter, *Stiftskirche*, pp. 194–239.

151. Schäfer, *Kanonissenstifter*, pp. 269–273.

CHAPTER FOUR:

VITA SANCTÆ

152. *Vita,* c. 3.

153. See Chapters 2 and 3 for details on Anno of Cologne and Bertha's relationship to him.

154. See also Groeteken, *Die heilige Adelheid,* pp. 7–27. In spite of the author's fanciful language and images, some of his comments about Adelheid and her life and times have proved insightful.

155. One famous example was certainly Einhard, *Vita Caroli,* which quoted extensively from Suetonius' *Life of Augustus.* Interestingly, Einhard was used as a model for a twelfth-century life of William the Conqueror, thus borrowing the Latin of Suetonius at second hand. The unique qualities of the individual being described have become ritualised within an ideal presentation of a royal presence.

156. See Hippolyte Delahaye, *The Legends of the Saints* trans. M. Crawford (1907; Bismarck ND: University of North Dakota Press, 1961 and Donald Weinstein and Rudolph M. Bell, *Saints and Society, 1000–1700* (Chicago: University of Chicago Press, 1982).

157. See Life of Bruno of Cologne; Bernward of Hildesheim; Ulrich of Augsburg and others. See Chapter 2, nn. 48; 58; 59.

158. *Vita,* c. 3.

159. See Chapter 2 and Groeteken, *Die heilige Adelheid,* pp. 29–42.

160. The canonical age for an abbess was apparently forty. This rule was more honoured in the breach than the observance and cannot be used to estimate the age of Adelheid. Compare for instance Otto I's daughter, Mathilda of Quedlinburg, who succeeded her grandmother as abbess in 968: she was born in 955. See also Chapter 3, n. 112.

161. See Chapter 2, n. 53 and Groeteken, *Die heilige Adelheid,* pp. 43–57.

162. *Vita,* c. 3.

163. *Vita,* c. 3. See also Groeteken, *Die heilige Adelheid,* pp. 58–68.

164. *Vita,* c. 3. See also *Inst. sanct.* VI and Tim 2:9.

165. *Vita,* c. 3.

166. *M.G.h.* DOIII 32,18 January, 987. Achter, *Stiftskirche,* gives the text of all the charters (pp. 333–335). See also *Jahrbücher des deutschen Reiches unter Otto II und Otto III,* Vol. 2, pp. 78–79.

167. Lacomblet, *Urkundenbuch* I, no. 126, p. 77. See also Groeteken, *Die heilige Adelheid,* pp. 69–86.

168. *M.G.h.* DHII 40, 26 February 26, 1003: " Nostro quoque tempore venerabilis eiusdem monasterii abbatissa nomine Adelheyda per interventum dilecte coniugis nostre Cunegunde videlicet regine nostra id denuo fieri munificencia supplex rogavit." Adolf of Nassau was an ill-fated anti-king against a Habsburg claimant, but Nassau is near both Geldern and Vilich and the convent would have been of interest to him.

169. In the Papal bull of 996, permission is granted for the introduction of the Benedictine Rule. See Achter, *Stiftskirche,* p. 333.

170. *Vita,* c. 3.

171. The influence upon Bertha came from her brother Wolfhelm, abbot of Brauweiler who had contact with the reform movements which originated at Cluny but also at the monastery of St. Vannes near Rheims. Vilich's history first as a house of canonesses; then as a Benedictine cloister, and finally, in the late middle ages, as a *weltlicher Stift* (canonesses again) is not without scholarly dispute. Oediger, *Geschichte des Erzbischoftums Köln,* Vol. 1. pp. 399–405 is strongly in favour of the Benedictine conversion; Achter, *Stiftskirche,* pp. 21–24 and n. 114 notes that on July 5, 1488, Pope Innocent VIII confirmed Vilich's status as a "secular abbey" (*weltlicher Stift*). The original charter is in the Staatsarchiv Düsseldorf, Stift Vilich, doc. 109. See also Chapter 3, n. 98.

172. Vita, c. 4.

173. *Vita,* c. 6.

174. See Achter, *Stiftskirche,* pp. 139–140 and pp. 293–300 on the remains of the burials. Groeteken, *Die heilige Adelheid,* pp. 87–97. See Chapter 3.

175. *Vita,* c. 5, 6. Groeteken, *Die heilige Adelheid,* pp. 98–118 for a fanciful description of Adelheid's work at Vilich and Cologne. See also Achter, *Stiftskirche,* p. 242, for a succinct comment on Vilich's history after 1804.

176. *Vita,* c. 6

177. See *Jahrbücher des deutschen Reiches unter Heinrich II* Vol. 1, pp. 193–242; Vol. 3, pp. 1–14 for details.

178. For details of the Aachen diet, see *Jahrbücher unter Otto II und Otto III,* Vol. 2, pp. 330–337. See also Chapter 2.

179. *Vita* of Heribert of Cologne written by Lautbert, *M.G.h.* SS IV, 745 ff.

180. *Vita,* c. 6.

181. *Vita,* c. 6.

182. *Vita,* c. 6.

183. *Vita,* c. 6

184. What follows is recorded by Bertha in *Vita,* c. 7.

185. *Vita,* c. 7. See also Groeteken, *Die heilige Adelheid,* pp. 119–135.

186. *Vita,* c. 11

187. *Vita,* c. 12–13

188. This has been described as "Little's Disease" named after William John Little (1810–1894), a British physician and surgeon. *Taber's Cyclopedic Medical Dictionary* describes it as follows: "Congenital spastic paralysis on both sides (diplegia), although it may also be paraplegic or heniplegic in form. Symptoms: child may be delayed in developing sphincter control and is usually mentally normal. Stiff awkward movements, legs crossed and pressed together, arms adducted, forearms flexed, hands pronated, sissors gait. Unknown cause, but possibly associated with prematurity or inadequate care of premature infant."

189. Achter, *Stiftskirche*, p. 281, n. 70. For another commentary on the miracles, see Groeteken, *Die heilige Adelheid*, pp. 136–150. At a later time, miracles began to occur at the Pützchen-Brünnlein, a fountain of healing water. For some comments see Achter, *Stiftskirche*, pp. 306–321 and Groeteken, *Die heilige Adelheid*, pp. 151–171.

190. *Vita*, c. 4.

191. *Vita*, c. 7. The biblical reference is to 1 Cor 7:7.

192. *Vita*, c. 7.

193. *Vita*, c. 7.

194. See J. Schlafke, "Verehrung der heiligen Adelheid im Laufe der Geschichte bis auf unsere Zeit." in Achter, *Stiftskirche*, pp. 293–329.

CHAPTER FIVE:

A *CAUSE CÉLÈBRE*

195. See Chapter 2, n. 88. The history of the manuscript is discussed in the Appendix.

196. That does not negate the local religious interest in Adelheid as a saint or the efforts which produced the post-World War II restoration of the Vilich church. See Albert Groeteken, *Die heilige Adelheid von Vilich und ihre Familie,* published in 1937. A second edition appeared in 1956 with the title, *Adelheid von Vilich Herrin und Magd.*

197. See Chapter 2 n. 45 and entries in the *Neue Deutsche Biographie* for biographies and bibliographical notes on the leading participants.

198. Holtzmann, *Geschichte der sächsischen Kaiserzeit,* pp. 468–473.

199. *Annales Quedlinburgenses,* SS III, 85ff.

200. Thietmar, *Chronicon* VIII. 7. Otto of Hammerstein was the first cousin of Thietmar's mother Kunigunde, daughter of Judith,

a sister of Otto's father Heribert Count of the Wetterau, who were the children of Udo, (†949), a member of the Conradin family. See Genealogical Tables.

201. See Chapter 2.

202. The Synod and Diet of Nymwegen are discussed in Thietmar, *Chronicon* VIII, 7; *Jahrbücher unter Heinrich II*, Vol. 3, pp. 72–73; Kessler, *Eheprozess*, pp. 44–46, Holtzmann, *Geschichte der sächsischen Kaiserzeit*, pp. 500ff; S. Reicke, "Der Hammersteiner Ehehandel," pp. 214–215.

203. Kessler, *Eheprozess*, pp. 17–44; Reicke, "Der Hammersteiner Ehehandel," pp. 209–212 on consanguinity and canon law.

204. Thietmar, *Chronicon* VIII, 18. *Jahrbücher unter Heinrich II*, Vol. 3, pp. 73; Kessler, *Eheprozess*, 46–47; Holtzmann, *Geschichte der sächsichen Kaiserzeit*, p. 514.

205. *Vita*, c. 3.

206. *Jahrbücher unter Heinrich II*, Vol. 3, pp. 267–272; Excursus IX, pp. 349–55. The text comes from a document in the Vatican library.

207. Kessler, *Eheprozess*, pp. 5–17 on the older scholarship; more recently Hlawitschka, *Anfänge des Hauses Habsburg-Lothringen*, pp. 45–70.

208. Through his father Heribert Otto was connected to the Conradin family whose position as dukes of Swabia and claimants to Franconia made them dangerous to the Ottonians. But Otto was also related to the family of Otto of Worms Duke of Carinthia. As Henry II had no children, this family, the Salians, were the heirs at law for succession of the empire. Otto of Worms was the son of Conrad the Red and Liudgard, the daughter of Otto I. It is possible that Conrad the Red was also a member of the Conradin family. See Hansmartin Schwarzmaier, *Von Speyer nach Rom* (Sigmaringer: Jan Thorbeke Verlag, 1991) for a discussion. Otto von Hammerstein's connection came through his maternal grandmother, whose brother was the ancestor of Adelheid, wife of Henry of Speyer, a son of Otto of Worms. See Kessler, *Eheprozess*, pp. 60–69. See also Reicke, "Hammersteiner Ehehandel." Henry II

may also have distrusted Irmingard of Hammerstein for her relationship to the Luxemburg family, Henry's unruly in-laws.
Siegfried of Luxemburg, Kunigunde's father, was the maternal
uncle of Irmingard's father Godfrey the Prisoner. For another view
on the Hammerstein affair and Henry II's conception of the
empire, see Giesebrecht, *Geschichte der deutsche Kaiserzeit,* Vol. 2,
pp. 1–205. Other factors may also have involved the position of
Archbishop Aribo of Mainz as primate of Germany and his opposition to the resurgence of papal power and the monastic reform
movements that had begun in Cluny, but were more recently
involved with Richard of St. Vannes and his followers, among
whom were prominent members of Irmingard's family. See also
Chapter 2, n. 86, 87.

209. *Ann. Quedl.* SS III, 85ff.; *Jahrbücher unter Heinrich II,* Vol. 3,
p. 172; Kessler, *Eheprozess,* p. 47.

210. The dates of the siege are confirmed by Henry II's charters
which are dated from the Hammerstein. *M.G.h.* DHII, nos. 434,
435, 436; *Jahrbücher unter Heinrich II,* Vol. 3, pp. 171–175; Kessler,
Eheprozess, pp. 47–51.

211. Aribo of Mainz in *Neue Biographie,* Vol. 1 with bibliography.

212. For Pilgrim see F. W. Oedinger, *Geschichte des Erzbistums
Köln,* Vol. 1, pp. 111–112.

213. This happened at the Council of Cologne at Pentecost,
June 2, 1023. See *Jahrbücher unter Heinrich II,* Vol. III, pp. 258–259;
Kessler, *Eheprozess,* pp. 51–52.

214. Kessler, *Eheprozess,* pp. 52–59. The canons of Seligenstadt,
particularly canon 16 and 18, refer to her unprecedented action
with loathing. Aribo of Mainz had tried to restrict free access to
the papacy by decreeing that no one could so appeal unless they
had his permission. Benedict VIII would have none of that and
the fight was on. When Aribo proved difficult, Benedict VIII
refused to grant him the pallium, the symbol of his episcopal
power. *Jahrbücher unter Henrich II,* Vol. 3, pp. 267–272, Excursus
IX, pp. 349–355. It is interesting to note that Ezzo, Count
Palatine of Aachen, and his wife, Princess Mathilda, were also in

Rome at this this time, seeking papal approval for their foundation at Brauweiler.

215. At the council of Frankfurt, 1027 Aribo tried to reopen the matter. See Kessler, *Eheprozess,* p. 59.

216. Udo's death in 1034 and Otto's in 1036 are recorded in the *Annales Necrologici Fuldenses M.G.h.* SS XIII, Codex I, Annus 1036 "Otto comes," p. 212.

217. Irmingard's death in recorded in the necrology of St. Vannes. See also Chapter 2.

APPENDIX

218. For a discussion of rhymed prose in Latin literature see Eduard Norden, *Die antike Kunstprosa vom VI. Jahrhundert v. Chr. bis zur Zeit der Renaissance* Vol. 2. 5th. ed. (Darmstadt: Wissenschaftliche Buchgesellschaft, 1958), pp. 705–711; Max Manitius, *Geschichte der lateinischen Litteratur des Mittelalters* 2 (München: Becksche Verlagsbuchhandlung, 1923), pp. 415, 469–47.

219. For the translation of this chapter, see Chapter 1.

220. Although the *vita* is well known to scholars and praised as a well-written Latin work of the eleventh century and recognised as a valuable historical source, there is very little discussion of Bertha and her work in the standard works on literature or history. See Wattenbach-Holtzmann, *Geschichtsquellen,* Vol. 2, pp. 668, 673. Giesebrecht, *Geschichte der deutschen Kaiserzeit,* Vol. 2, pp. 545–546 for some succinct comments on education for women in the tenth and early eleventh centuries. See also Herbert Grundmann, "Die Frauen und die Litteratur im Mittelalter; Ein Beitrag nach der Entstehung des Schrifttums in der Volkssprache" *Ausgewählte Schriften* 3: *Schriften der Monumenta Germaniæ Historica* 25 (1978), pp. 67–95.

221. See *Vita,* c. 3.

222. See n. 88.

223. In Chapter 3, Bertha quotes from the Wisdom of Solomon: " . . . quæ, ut habetur in scriptis, talibus prophetæ commendatur dictis: 'Senectus veneralilis non diuturna neque numero annorum computata' . . . . The original reads "Senectus enim venerabilis est non diuturna neque numero annorum computata . . . ." For a translation, see Chapter 1.

224. Wilhelm Levison, "Conspectus Codicum hagiographicorum," *Monumenta Germaniæ Historica in rerum Scriptorum Merowingicorum* VII, 2 (Hannover: Hahn, 1920), pp. 537–538. This is a listing of the location of hagiographical manuscripts arranged alphabetically by city, as located in 1920.

225. Included in the legendary are Fortunatus's *vitæ* of St. Hilary and St. Radegunde, the lives of St. Boniface, St. Remigius, St. Willibrord, St. Cuthbert, St. Columbanus, Germanus, Wenceslaus, Geneviève and Waldburga, as well as Gregory of Tours' *Miracles of St. Andrew.* See Levison, pp. 562–563, 604–605.

226. Bruxel. MS 98–100, "memb. folio maximi, sæc. XIII. in., partis magni cuiudam legendarii acta sanctorum mensium Junii–Septembris contimentis, inter quæ f. 220–223. Vitam Adelheidis."

227. Laurentius Surius, *De probatis sanctororium historiis.* 2nd. ed. 1576; printed editions 1581 and 1618. See Achter, *Stiftskirche,* pp. 263–265.

228. Jean Mabillon and Lucas d'Achery, *Acta sanctorum Ordinis Sancti Benedicti in saeculorum classis distributa* (Paris, 1668–1701). 9 vols.

229. British Museum, Dept. of Manuscripts, *Catalogue of the Harleian Manuscripts in the British Museum,* Art. 2800. See also Levison, "Conspectus," pp. 537, 603–605.

Bibliography

Primary Sources

Bauer, Albert and Reinhold Bau, *Quellen zur Geschichte der sächsischen Kaiserzeit.* Darmstadt: Wissenschaftliche Buchgesellschaft, 1971.

Benedict, Saint. *RB 1980: The Rule of St. Benedict in Latin and English, with Notes.* Ed. Timothy Fry. Collegeville MN; The Liturgical Press, 1981.

—"The Benedictine Rule" in Donald A. White, *Medieval History, A Sourcebook.* Homeward, Ill.: Dorsey Press, 1965, pp. 139–179.

Bible. *Revised Standard Version.* New York: Thomas Nelson and Sons, 1953.

Bible. *Old Testament Apocrypha.* Trans. Edgar J. Goodspeed. Chicago: University of Chicago Press, 1938.

British Museum. Dept. of Manuscripts. *A Catalogue of the Harleian Manuscripts in the British Museum.* London: B. Eyre and A. Strahan, 1808–1812.

Caesarius of Arles. *Rule for Nuns.* Trans. by Mother Maria Caritas McCarthy. Washington DC: The Catholic University Press, 1960.

Cyprian. *Treatises.* Trans. and ed. Roy J. Deferrari. New York: Fathers of the Church Inc., 1958.

Eusebius. *The History of the Church from Christ to Constantine.* Trans. C.A. Williamson. Harmondsworth: Penguin Books, 1965.

Jerome. *Letters and Select Works.* Trans. W.H. Freemantle, with the assistance of G. Lewis and W.G. Martley. Nicene and Post-Nicene Fathers of the Christian Church, series 2, Vol. 6. Oxford: Parker, 1893.

Kallfelz, Hatto. *Lebensbeschreibungen einiger Bischofe des 10. bis 12. Jahrhundert.* Darmstadt: Wissenschaftliche Buchgesellschaft, 1973.

Lacomblet, Theodor. *Urkundenbuch für die Geschichte des Niederrheins.* Vol. 1. 1840. Aalen: Scientia Verlag, 1960.

Liudprand of Cremona. *Works.* London: Routledge, 1930.

Mommsen, Theodor Ernst and Carl Morrison. *Imperial Lives and Letters of the Eleventh Century.* New York: Columbia University Press, 1962.

Monumenta Germania historica. Diplomatum regum et imperatorum Germaniae. Vols. II and III. Hannover: Hahnsche Buchhandlung, 1893, 1900-1903.

Monumenta Germania historica. Constitutiones et Acta Publica imperatorum et regum. Vol. I. Hannover: Hahnsche Buchhandlung, 1893.

Monumenta Germaniae historica. Legem Sectio III. Concilia: Vol. II. *Concilia Aevi Karolini* I. Ed. Albert Werminghoff. Hannover: Hahnsche Buchhandlung, 1906.

Monumenta Germaniae historica. Scriptores. Vol. I.ff. Hannover: Hanhnsche Buchhandlung, 1826ff.

Odilonis Cluniacensis abbatis Epitaphium domine Adelheide auguste. Monumenta Germania historica. Scriptores IV (1841), pp. 636-649.

—Ed. Herbert Paulhart. *Mitteilungen des Instituts für österreichische Geschichte, Ergänzungsband* 20/2. Festschrift für Jahrtausendfeier der Kaiserkrönung Otto des Grossen, 2 (1962); translations in *Geschichtsschreiber der deutschen Vorzeit 10. Jahrhundert* Vol. 8. (Berlin, 1856); Vol. 35. 2nd ed. (Leipzig, 1891).

Pabst, Herman. "Die Brauweiler Geschichtsquellen" *Archiv der Gesellschaft für altere deutsche Geschichtskunde* 12 (1858–1874), pp. 80ff.

Die Statuten von Santa Maria im Kapitol. Ed. K.H. Schafer. *Inventäre und Regesten aus dem Kölner Pfarrarchiven* 3; *Annalen des historischen Vereins für den Niederrhein* 70 (1901), 76 (1903), 83 (1907).

Sylvester II: The Letters of Gerbert of Aurillac. Trans. Harriet Pratt Lattin. New York: Columbia University Press, 1961.

Thietmar von Merseburg. *Chronik.* Trans. Werner Trillman. Berlin: Deutscher Verlag der Wissenschaften, 1966.

Vita Adelheidis abbatissae Vilicensis auctore Bertha. Ed. D. Holder-Egger. *Monumenta Germania historica, SS.* XV. 754ff.

—*Leben und Verehrung der heiligen Adelheid von Vilich.* Trans. Jacob Schlafke. Irmingard Achter. *Die Siftskirche St. Peter in Vilich.* Die Kunstdenkmaler des Rheinlandes 52. Düsseldorf: Rheinland Verlag, 1968.

Secondary Sources

Achter, Irmgard. *Die Stiftskirche St. Peter in Vilich and Jacob Schlafke, Leben und Verehrung der heiligen Adelheid von Vilich.* Die Kunstdenkmaler des Rheinlandes, Beiheft 52. Düsseldorf: Rheinland Verlag, 1968.

Bäumer, Gertrud. *Otto I und Adelheid.* Tübingen und Stuttgart: Rainer Wunderlich Verlag, 1951.

Bäumer, Gertrud. *Adelheid Mutter der Konigreiche.* Tübingen: Rainer Wunderlich Verlag, 1936.

Bresslau, Harry. "Otto von Hammerstein und sein Haus." *Forschungen zur deutschen Geschichte* 21 (1881): 401ff.

Coens, Maurice. "Une fiction d'origine rhénan: S. Suibert,

évêque-martyre de Bethléem. *Analecta Bollandiana* 56 (1948): 91–117.

Delahaye, Hippolyte. *The Legends of the Saints.* Introd. Richard Schoek. Trans. M. Crawford. 1907. Place: University of North Dakota, 1961.

Dick, Madelyn Bergen. "The Empress Adelheid: A Portrait Study from the Tenth Century." Paper presented at the 10th International Congress of Medieval Studies, the Medieval Institute, Western Michigan University, Kalamazoo, Michigan, May 1975.

Dick, Madelyn Bergen. "Colloquium Dominarum: Political Activity of Aristocratic Women in Ottonian Germany." Paper presented at the 23rd International Congress of Medieval Studies, the Medieval Institute, Western Michigan University, Kalamazoo, Michigan, 7 May, 1988.

Diwalt, Helmut. *Heinrich der Erste.* Bergisch Gladbach: Gustav Lubbe Verlag, 1987.

Duckett, Eleanor S. *Anglo-Saxon Saints and Scholars.* Hamden: Archon Books, 1967.

Erler, Mary and Maryanne Kkowaleski, eds. *Women and Power in the Middle Ages.* Athens: University of Georgia Press, 1988.

Fichtenau, Heinrich. *Living in the Tenth Century: Mentalities and Social Orders.* Trans. Patrick J. Geary. Chicago: University of Chicago Press, 1992.

Franz, Hildegard. "Die Marken Valenciennes-Eename und Antwerpen im Rahmen der kaiserlichen Grenzsicherungspolitik and der Schelde im 10. und 11. Jahrhundert." *Rheinische Vierteljahrblatter* 10 (1940): 229–276.

Giesebrecht, Wilhelm von. *Geschichte der deutschen Kaiserzeit.* 5 vols. Braunschweig: Schwetschke, 1881.

Greenway, George William. *Saint Boniface; Three Biographical*

Studies. London: A and C. Black, 1955.

Groeteken, Albert. *Die heilige Adelheid von Vilich und ihre Familie*. Kevelaer: Verlag Butzon und Bercker, 1937.

Grundmann, Herbert. "Die Frauen und die Litteratur im Mittelalter; Ein Beitrag nach der Entstehung des Schrifttums in der Volkssprache." *Ausgewählte Schriften* vol. 3. *Schriften der Monumenta Germaniae Historica* 25 (1978): 67–95.

Gümbel, Helmut. *Sankt Adelheid von Vilich: Zur Geschichte ihres Lebens, ihres Wirkens, und ihres Kloster*. Studien zur Heimatsgeschichte der Stadt Beuel am Rhein, 8. Beuel: City of Beuel, 1965.

Hiller, Helmut. *Otto der Grosse und seine Zeit*. München: List Verlag, 1980.

Hirsch, Siegfried. *Jahrbücher des deutschen Reiches unter Heinrich II*. 3 vols. Ed. Harry Bresslau. Berlin: Duncker and Humblot, 1862–1875.

Hlawitschka, Eduard. *Die Anfänge des Hauses Habsburg-Lothringen und des Reiches im 9. und 10. Jahrhundert*. Saarbrucken: Minerva Verlag, 1969.

Holtzmann, Robert. *Geschichte der sächsischen Kaiserzeit*. 1941. München: Verlag Georg D. W. Callway, 1961.

Hubinger, Paul Egon. "Oberlothringen, Rhein und Reich im Hochmittelalter: Umriß und Aufgaben." *Rheinische Vierteljahrblatter* 7 (1937): 141–160.

Hughes, Andrew. *Medieval Manuscripts for Mass and Office: A Guide to their Organization and Terminology*. Toronto: University of Toronto Press, 1982.

Jenal, Georg. *Erzbischof Anno II von Köln (1056–1075) und sein politisches Werken*. 2 vols. Stuttgart: Anton Hiersemann, 1974.

Kaiserin Theophanu: Prinzessin aus der Fremde des Westreiches Große Kaiserin. Ed. Gunther Wolf et al. Köln: Böhlau

Verlag, 1991.

Kempen, E. "Rheinische Anfänge des Hauses Habsburg-Lothringen." *Annalen des Historischen Vereins für den Niederrhein* 23 (1933): 22ff.

Kessler, Dorothea von. *Der Eheprozess Ottos und Irmingards von Hammerstein.* Ebering's Historische Studien 157. Berlin: Ebering, 1923.

Klueting, Edeltraut. *Das Bistum Osnabruck. Germania Sacra: Die Bistumer der Kirchenprovinz Koln,* N.F. 21. Köln, 1986.

Lewald, Ursula. "Die Ezzonen." *Rheinische Vierteljahrblatter: Mitteilungen für Geschichtliche Landeskunde des Rheinlandes an der Universität Bonn* 43 (1979): 120-168.

Leyser, K.J. *Rule and Conflict in an Early Medieval Society: Ottonian Saxony.* Bloomington: Indiana University Press, 1979.

Manitius, Max. *Geschichte der Lateinischen Litteratur des Mittelalters.* 3 vols. München: Becksche Verlagsbuchhandlung, 1923.

Martimort, Aimé Georges. *Deaconesses: An Historical Study.* San Francisco: Ignatius Press, 1986.

McKitterick, Rosamund. *The Frankish Kingdoms under the Carolingians.* London: Longman, 1983.

McKitterick, Rosamund. "Ottonian Intellectual Culture in the Tenth Century and the Role of Theophanu." *Early Medieval Europe* 2 (1993): 53–74.

Mikoletzky, Hanns Leo. *Kaiser Heinrich II. und die Kirche.* Wien: Universum, 1946.

Neue Biographie. Berlin: Duncker & Humblot, 1952ff.

New Catholic Encyclopedia. Toronto: McGraw-Hill, 1967.

Norden, Eduard. *Die Antike Kunstprosa vom VI. Jahrhundert v. Chr. bis zur Zeit der Renaissance.* 2 vols. 5th. ed. Darmstadt:

Wissenschaftliche Buchgesellschaft, 1958.

Oediger, Friedrich Wilhelm. *Vom Leben am Niederrhein.* Düsseldorf: Pädagogischer Verlag Schwann, 1973.

Oediger, Friedrich Wilhelm. *Geschichte des Erzbistums Köln.* Vol. 1. *Das Bistum Köln von den Anfängen bis zum Ende des 12. Jahrhunderts.* 2nd ed. Köln: Verlag J. P. Bachem, 1972.

Polheim, Karl. *Die Lateinische Reimprosa.* Berlin: Weidmannsche Verlagsbuchhandlung, 1963 (1925).

Reicke, Siegfried. "Der Hammersteiner Ehehandel im Lichte der mittelalterlichen Herrschaftsordnung." Ed. Ursula Lewald. *Rheinische Vierteljahresblatter* 38 (1974): 203–224.

Reuter, Timothy. *Germany in the Early Middle Ages.* London: Longman, 1991.

Schäfer, K. Heinrich. *Die Kanonissenstifter im deutschen Mittelalter.* 1907. Amsterdam: P. Schippers N.V., 1965.

Schröer, Alois. *Die Kirche in Westfalen vor der Reformation.* Münster: Aschendorff, 1967.

Schmidt, Tilman. "Kaiser Konrad II: Jugend und Familie." *Geschichtsschreibung und geistiges Leben: Festschrift Heinz Löwe.* Köln: Bohlau, 1978, 312-324.

Schwarzmaier, Hansmartin. *Von Speyer nach Rom.* Sigmaringer: Jan Thorbeke Verlag, 1991.

Sproemberg, Heinrich. "Die lothringische Politik Otto des Grossen." *Rheinische Vierteljahrblatter* XI (1941): 1–101.

Sutherland, J.D. "The Mission of Liudprand of Cremona". *Traditio* 31 (1975): 55–81.

Thomas, Clayton L. *Taber's Cyclopedic Medical Dictionary.* 16th ed. Philadelphia: F.A. Davis and Co., 1989.

Uhlirz, Mathilda. "Studien uber Theophanu: I und II." *Deutsches Archiv* 6 (1943): 442-474.

Uhlirz, Karl und Mathilde. *Jahrbücher des deutschen Reiches unter Otto II und Otto III.* 2 vols. 2nd ed. Berlin: Duncker und Humblot, 1967.

Wattenbach, Wilhelm-Robert Holtzmann. *Deutschland's Geschichtsquellen im Mittelalter: Die Zeit der Sachsen und Salier.* Ed. Franz Josef Schmale. 3 vols. Köln: Bohlaus Verlag, 1967.

Weigel, Helmut. "Aufbau und Wandlungen der Grundherrschaft des Frauenstiftes Essen (852–1803)." *Das erste Jahrtausend.* Vol. I. Ed. Victor E. Elbern. Düsseldorf: Verlag L. Schwann, 1962. 256–295.

Weinstein, Donald and Rudolph M. Bell. *Saints and Society (1000-1700).* Chicago: University of Chicago Press, 1982.

Werminghoff, Albert, "Die Beschlüsse des Aachener Conzils im Jahre 816", *Neues Archiv,* 27 (1902), pp. 605–675.

Wimmer, Franz Paul. *Kaiserin Adelheid, Gemahlin Ottos I des Grossen in ihrem Leben und Wirken von 931–973.* Regensburg: J. Habbel, 1897.

Wisplinhoff, Erich. "Zur Frühgeschichte von Vilich." *Rheinische Vierteljahrblatter* 18 (1953): 78-83.